Think SOLD!

Creating Home Sales in Any Market

Tammy Lynch,
CSP, CMP, MIRM

BuilderBooks.com®
BOOKS THAT BUILD YOUR BUSINESS

A Service of

NAHB®
NATIONAL ASSOCIATION
OF HOME BUILDERS

Think Sold! Creating Home Sales in Any Market

BuilderBooks, a Service of the National Association of Home Builders

Courtenay S. Brown	Director, Book Publishing
Natalie C. Holmes	Book Editor
Tracy Quinn McLennan	Copy Editor
Torrie M. Singletary	Production Editor
Circle Graphics	Cover Design
Circle Graphics	Composition
P.A. Hutchison	Printing
Gerald M. Howard	NAHB Executive Vice President and CEO
Mark Pursell	NAHB Senior Vice President, Marketing & Sales Group
Lakisha Campbell	NAHB Vice President, Publications & Affinity Programs

Disclaimer

This publication provides accurate information on the subject matter covered. The publisher is selling it with the understanding that the publisher is not providing legal, accounting, or other professional service. If you need legal advice or other expert assistance, obtain the services of a qualified professional experienced in the subject matter involved. Reference herein to any specific commercial product, process, or service by trade name, trademark, manufacturer, or otherwise does not necessarily constitute or imply endorsement, recommendation, or favored status by the National Association of Home Builders. The views and opinions of the author expressed in this publication do not necessarily state or reflect those of the National Association of Home Builders, and they shall not be used to advertise or endorse a product.

Printed in the United States of America

12 11 10 09   1 2 3 4 5

ISBN-10: 0-86718-653-4
ISBN-13: 978-0-86718-653-6

Library of Congress Cataloging-in-Publication Data

Lynch, Tammy, 1964-
  Think sold! : creating home sales in any market / Tammy Lynch.
     p. cm.
  Includes bibliographical references and index.
  ISBN-13: 978-0-86718-653-6
  ISBN-10: 0-86718-653-4
  1. House selling. 2. Real estate business. 3. Salesmen and salesmanship. I. Title.

HD1379.L96 2009
333.33'83—dc22

2009011855

For further information, please contact:

National Association of Home Builders
1201 15th Street, NW
Washington, DC 20005-2800
800-223-2665
Visit us online at www.BuilderBooks.com.

Contents

About the Author

*T*ammy Lynch CSP, CMP, MIRM, is a successful real estate broker, consultant, and owner of Lynch Consulting, Inc./ Results Source (www. resultssource.com), in Bradenton, Florida. She is a certified building contractor who specializes in sales training and coaching. Ms. Lynch is a certified principal instructor for the University of Housing for the following Institute for Residential Marketing (IRM) courses: Understanding Housing Markets and Consumers and Marketing Strategies, Plans, and Budgets; and for the Master Certified Marketing Professional (MCMP) course, House Construction as a Selling Tool.

The first female president of the Home Builders Association of Manatee, Florida, Ms. Lynch also has received many home building industry achievement awards. She is a life director of the Tampa Bay Builders Association, trustee of the IRM 2004–2007, builder director for the National Association of Home Builders (NAHB) since 2005, past president of the Florida Home Builders Foundation, and a member of the National Sales and Marketing Council as well as the Greater Tampa, Sarasota, and National Associations of Realtors.

Ms. Lynch's passion is being able to speak to groups about how faith and belief in the power within can change lives. She has authored a book on the subject—*Today's Master Key*—and is the co-author of *The Mastery of Abundant Living: The Key to Mastering the Law of Attraction*, *The Mastery of Abundant Living: The Magical Thinking of the Law of Attraction*, and *The Mastery of Abundant Living: Christian Keys to the Law of Attraction*.

Foreword

*I*first met Tammy Lynch during a housing trough. It was 1992 and a large national home builder had asked me to analyze why home sales in some of its communities were nearly twice those in its other communities. At the time, homes were not viewed as a good financial investment. Home appreciation was trailing the Consumer Price Index and interest rates averaged more than 8%. The Resolution Trust Corporation (RTC) was busy dumping home sites on the market from bankrupt developers. Newspaper headlines said that home prices would decline before the real estate market would recover. In short, home selling was a competitive business in which you had to fight for every closing.

Tammy was a field sales manager at the time and had shown significant sales improvement in a number of communities for which she was responsible. I called Tammy and peppered her with questions to try to ascertain why she was so successful.

"Tell me about your traffic," I said.

"I'll fax you the graphs and we can discuss," she replied.

"What about return visitors?"

"I'll send that as well," she said.

As we continued talking, I realized that she not only had the answer to each question but that she was always looking underneath the sales numbers to uncover the keys to motivating both salespeople and home buyers. After talking to Tammy, I had but one recommendation for my home builder client: "Clone Tammy Lynch and put her in every sales office!"

Tammy's sales philosophy is surprisingly simple: Salespeople gain confidence through knowledge and attitude. Unless you know your competitors, you cannot properly present your product and speak confidently about your pricing. Without knowledge of the features of a home, you're unable to show it in its best possible light. Without the knowledge gained through customer follow-up, you will never understand why you lost a sale. And, most importantly, without the knowledge of solid selling skills, you will never be able to uncover the underlying buying motivations needed to match your homes to the needs of your buyers.

Sales skills have never been more important to a builder's success. At the same time, the sales process is more sophisticated today than in the past. Salespeople must be better prepared and more skilled. I say this because the Internet has made our customers more knowledgeable about the housing market than ever.

Yet, with the unprecedented housing boom of the last decade, many salespeople became mere order takers. Consequently, today's new home sales professionals are among the least likely to have received the kind of quality training and reinforcement needed to succeed in a tough market. Twelve consecutive years of increased sales volume and home price appreciation that eclipsed the rate of inflation made the industry take sales, and the role of the sales professional, for granted. During this time, it was not uncommon for well-meaning managers to focus on the administrative tasks of a sales team such as perfect paperwork and on-time attendance at sales meetings at the expense of their mastering selling skills.

Consider the state of the world at the time of the last real estate low point in 1992:

- The Internet was unknown and had yet to become commercially viable.
- The average baby boomer was 36—the prime age for seeking a move-up home.

- Average commuting time was 24% shorter than it is today.
- Home affordability was 41% greater than it is today.

Consumers have changed. Today's customers do not want to be sold a home. They want to be assisted with the buying process. They are more informed and educated about new home communities. You can bet that they know as much about your competitors as you do, yet they will test you when comparing communities to see if home builders will beat others' prices, regardless of home features and quality. Customers are looking for a true sales counselor to assist them instead of a slick sales agent who constantly tries to spin what customers know are legitimate concerns in buying a new home.

Think Sold! Creating Home Sales in Any Market reveals not only the fundamentals of new home selling skills, it also provides insight into the self motivation needed in a world where rejection is an everyday occurrence. Few sales trainers are as skilled as Tammy Lynch in bridging the gap between the theoretical and the practical in new home sales. She does this by showing salespeople how to first envision success in sales and then create a roadmap to realize that vision. This book is a must-read for anyone who is serious about improving their selling skills in the current real estate environment.

—John Rymer
President
New Home Knowledge
www.newhomeknowledge.com

Acknowledgments

*I*often reflect back on my career in the industry. Three individuals significantly impacted my path and my results. Because they believed in and supported me, I had the opportunity to develop my personal sales skills and learn how to present them to others in a motivating manner.

I am thankful to Vito Simplicio for training me early in my career. He is an exceptional trainer who had his associates memorize scripts for each aspect of the sales process. This type of discipline is essential to the success of any new home sales associate. But he taught me much more than scripts, and he was instrumental in grooming me as a successful vice president of sales and marketing.

Second, I thank Mike McElroy for being my mentor. In fact, he has positively influenced many, many new home sales professionals. Mike provided me with the foundation to be a strong leader, and without leadership skills, I would not have been able to gain the experience that has contributed significantly to my growth in the industry.

Finally, I am grateful for the opportunity to have worked with Mike Storey. When others doubted whether I could manage an entire home building operation, Mike believed in me.

Each of these exceptional people has touched my life and my career beyond what words could express. They also share a character trait that makes them heroes in this business: integrity. My success in the industry and *Think Sold!* are direct results of the knowledge they shared, their character, and the opportunities for growth they offered me.

Success and the "It" Factor

Success is not a destination but a journey toward the accomplishment of predetermined, worthwhile goals. The journey in sales isn't about learning basic skills. It's about being a change agent who strives for continuous improvement. It's about your education and growth as a whole person rather than just your sales techniques. And it's about your ability to go deep inside yourself to understand personalities, relationships with others, current circumstances, and your ability to create your destiny.

Think Sold! Creating Home Sales in Any Market will provide you with tools for ongoing success in the industry. You may be surprised to learn that these tools include not only presentation and demonstration skills but also visualization skills. Visualizing success is a precursor to achieving results in sales. It is a tool to aid you in controlling your thoughts and altering your beliefs to be success oriented and to put you in control of your work and your life. Regardless of the current housing market, interest rates, energy costs, or the overall economy, by controlling your thoughts and applying mental imagery along with the theories, techniques, and strategies outlined in this book, you can make the next decade in the industry your best ever.

"The people who get on in this world are the ones who get up and look for the circumstances they want and, if they can't find them, they make them."

—GEORGE BERNARD SHAW
Playwright

Everything you accomplish is governed by the following three immutable principles:

- Your beliefs are consistent with who you are.
- Who you *are* is shaped by what you *think*.
- You achieve only if you believe you can.

Your mental attitude and focus determine your success or failure. Define your purpose and focus on your goal and you will begin to plant the seeds of your success. The most powerful tool at your disposal is your imagination. Use it to reach your desired destiny. If you can dream and imagine, you can create without limitation.

You must develop constructive beliefs consciously and continually. Eventually the habit of focusing on positive thoughts, feelings, and outcomes will become automatic and as natural as breathing. As a result, you will succeed in sales, enjoy the work more, and have the life you want.

As in any profession, success in sales demands planning. The first step in the planning process is to decide who you want to become and what you want to achieve. Do you want to be the best new home sales associate in your company? Do you want to be the best in your market? Once you have established your goal, visualizing your plan for getting there will help you eventually reach it. In your imagination, you have no limitations except for those you impose upon yourself. Your power to think is unlimited, and therefore, your power to create the vision of your perfect reality is also unlimited. You must throw out all preconceived notions of what can and cannot be, and picture yourself executing perfectly every time.

Imagine that if you think, believe, and expect a result, it will happen. If you expect to be successful, you act as if you are successful, and your actions create success. A destructive thought, on the other hand, is your personal devil. Like a germ, it attacks from the inside and can weaken your resolve and interfere with your success. Your thoughts and beliefs have shaped and will continue to govern your life. If you are not happy, then you have adopted beliefs that are destructive or are not aligned with your true

desires, perhaps without even realiz-
ing it. You have used your power,
albeit unintentionally, to prevent
you from attaining your true desires.
Practice listening to your emotions.
If you feel bad about a situation,
that feeling is rooted in inconsistency between your thoughts and
your true desires. The bad feeling
is a siren warning you that danger is
approaching.

> You are the gatekeeper that protects your mind from negative, destructive thoughts. Replace them with positive, successful, empowering thoughts.

You are the gatekeeper that protects your mind from negative, destructive thoughts. Replace them with positive, successful, empowering thoughts
by practicing positive self-talk, visualization, and mental imagery.

Overcoming Fear

One of the most destructive emotions you can have is fear because
fear is the root of all other negative emotions. When you replace fear with
a more positive emotion, such as love, your reality will change significantly. When you are fearful, think courageously. If you find yourself
dwelling on what you don't have, retrain your mind to think of what
you're grateful for or what you have in abundance.

Are you willing to release your negative feelings? *Will* is the predom-
inant factor in your success or failure in any venture. Once you have
decided that you are willing to give up your fear, you have freed yourself to
change your life immediately or sometime in the future. Make no mistake;
this transformation is a matter of personal choice. If you decide now to
change your mind, you can.

To start changing now, try this exercise: When a destructive thought
enters your mind, close your eyes and take a deep breath and hold it.
Think about your fear and count slowly from one to three. When you get
to three, release the breath and imagine that as you exhale, the fear is
leaving your mind and body along with your breath. Open your eyes,
take a deep breath, and imagine, as you draw in air, a pleasurable experience or situation. Let that sensation fill your body and mind as the fresh
air fills your lungs. You can control your thoughts. By determining what

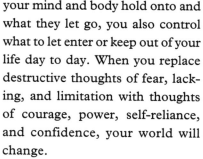

> "If you think you can do a thing or if you think you can't do a thing, you are right."
>
> —HENRY FORD
> *Inventor*

your mind and body hold onto and what they let go, you also control what to let enter or keep out of your life day to day. When you replace destructive thoughts of fear, lacking, and limitation with thoughts of courage, power, self-reliance, and confidence, your world will change.

I have been afraid, and I have overcome fear using these techniques. I know they work.

In December 1989 I married and by the following February I was pregnant. My son was due in November, but by October, I was already divorced. Naturally, I was anxious about the prospect of becoming a single mother. How would I take on this awesome responsibility on my own? In addition, as my brief marriage was dissolving, I was traveling frequently, selling bank card and check processing services to retailers. I knew my extensive travel would soon be out of the question and that I would need to make a career change. I had to make some difficult decisions.

Instead of fixating on the anxiety, however, I pictured my son and myself happy, healthy, and financially secure. I didn't know how this perfect picture would become reality; I just convinced myself that everything would be all right. Whenever there was inkling that things might not be okay, I redirected my thoughts to envision great pleasure and success. Using my mental powers, I'd begin to feel as if I had already accomplished this success. I didn't lose sight of my son and me stress-free and happy together in our home.

In fact, this American dream of homeownership was foremost in my mind as I was perusing the Help Wanted section of the newspaper one day. Amazingly, I came across an advertisement by U.S. Home for new home sales associates. I responded to the ad and soon joined U.S. Home as an on-site sales associate.

My first assignment with U.S. Home was in the community of Country Way in Plant City, Florida. In the previous six months, Country Way had two sales. But in my first 60 days, with no new home sales experience, I sold 6 homes. It was the beginning of the financially secure, happy life that I had envisioned.

Using Mental Imagery

The vivid mental imagery that I applied to reach my goals is really the first step to accomplishing anything in life, whether personally or professionally. Any new product, service, or invention is first imagined in the mind of its creator. Any great athlete or performer imagines their perfect time, execution, or performance prior to the event. Any great architect imagines a beautiful structure prior to sketching it on paper.

Jack Nicklaus, one of the all-time greatest golfers, said mental imagery was crucial to his success. "For some 40 years now, I've gone through the same visualization process before every competitive shot. No other discipline has helped me more . . . visualizing exactly what you want to achieve before setting up and swinging will greatly improve your play. The more deeply you ingrain what I like to call my 'going-to-the-movies' discipline, the more effective you will become at hitting the shots you want to hit."[1]

He explains this process in detail beginning with "seeing" in his mind where he wants the ball to finish. Then he "sees" the ball flying to the target he just visualized including the trajectory, curvature, and roll. Next, he "sees" himself setting up and swinging in such a way as to turn these visions into reality. And finally, he selects the club that will achieve his completed "movie" and steps up to the ball to execute the vision he just created.

Clearly, the subconscious mind does not differentiate between fiction and reality. Scientists agree that the human nervous system cannot tell the difference between an actual experience and an experience imagined vividly, emotionally, and in detail.[2] Therefore, you must have a clear, vivid picture of what you wish to achieve as a new home sales associate. Rather than focusing on how you will achieve your goal, focus first on the end result. Hold that image in your mind. You must savor the feeling of enjoying your results. You must imagine that you have already achieved your dream and are now living it. Then you can motivate yourself each day to consciously become the professional you want to be.

Conversely, if you constantly envision a bad end to what you perceive is a bad housing market, you will lose a sense of urgency with your prospects and the "bad market" will become a self-fulfilling prophesy. Your pessimism is the roadblock to achieving results. Even if a qualified prospect walks through the door, you won't recognize them because you've convinced yourself that there are no qualified prospects.

Instead, visualize perfect presentations and a wealth of qualified prospects, and your presentations will improve. Better presentations will lead to improved results. You will treat everyone as a qualified prospect; many of them will be, and many will buy your homes. Don't let your prospects' perceptions or prejudices cloud your belief that you are selling a wonderful product in a desirable community.

Imagine that you have unlimited resources and the power to attract anything and everything you desire. Imagine that you control every situation or circumstance in your life and there is nothing beyond your control. Now, stop imagining, and believe!

Creating Success

In 1992, I got an opportunity to sell homes in a new community, but it had two challenges. When you entered the neighborhood, among the first things you encountered were high-voltage power lines and an electrical substation. Also, a special school for children who needed emotional counseling abutted the community. Our competitors were using both of these location factors against us. Many sales associates didn't want to sell homes there.

With my vision of becoming a top seller firmly planted in my mind, though, I invited the local power company to visit and conduct tests that would provide me with the data to show to prospects fearful of electromagnetic fields (EMFs), the readings associated with the power lines and substation. We compared the readings to everyday living in a home that was not located near the power lines. We found that most people were exposed to higher readings of EMFs while in their family rooms watching television than what they would experience in the yards of the homes that backed up to the power lines.

I also visited the specialty school, which seemed more like an upscale boarding school than what our competitors were leading our prospects to believe. I obtained information about the school, the students attending, the adult-to-student ratio, and much more knowledge to overcome what our competition was saying about the school.

After I spoke with our prospects about these issues, many lost respect for my competitors' sales associates, who were spinning the data about our community rather than trying to inform and educate prospects. Ultimately,

I had great success in the community and achieved sales way beyond what the company had expected. If I had decided that external factors such as the community location features were roadblocks, I would have undermined my own success. Positive mental imagery helped me—and it will help you—develop self-confidence and allow you to pursue proactive strategies that will augment your selling before a prospect confronts you in the sales office.

Practicing Visualization

You may say you are still having trouble with visualization. When you close your eyes, all you see is darkness. In fact, many people find visualization difficult, but that's only because they are not familiar with it. Like playing a musical instrument, taking up tennis, or learning any other skill, visualization becomes easier with practice.

Try the following exercise: Picture someone special in your life right now. What does this person look like? What color is his or her hair and eyes? What is he or she wearing? Can you describe this person? If you can, then you already have the ability to visualize; you just need to practice and apply this skill daily.

Visualizing is much easier when you are completely relaxed. So, if you have difficulty visualizing, schedule time when you can relax and focus. I have found that immediately before I go to sleep is a good time to practice visualization. I actually schedule 20 to 30 minutes at night before I go to sleep to practice visualizing the immediate and long-term future. I picture the next day as well as the satisfaction of living my perfect life.

Try this exercise. Select a blank space on the wall (if you are sitting) or on the ceiling (if you are lying down). Mentally draw a black horizontal line about six inches long. See the line as plainly as if it were painted on the wall. Next, mentally draw two perpendicular lines to intersect this horizontal line. Then "draw" another horizontal line to make a square. Draw a circle within the square. Place a point in the center of the circle and draw the point toward you. You will see a cone on a square base.

Change the color of your lines from black to white, then red, then yellow. Now change the color to orange and rotate the cone so that you can now picture it standing on its base. If you can do this, you are making excellent progress and will soon be able to concentrate on any situation you desire. Eventually, with practice, you will begin to see more vivid pictures, and you can substitute this simple picture for ones with more detail.

Let's move on to something more advanced. Get a photograph of someone in your life who you love immensely. Study the photograph carefully. Make note of each feature, including the color and shape of this person's eyes. Close your eyes and completely relax. Now, see your loved one in your mind but with the same level of detail. Can you picture this person? If so, that's awesome! You are well on your way to being able to use the power of visualization. If you're not there yet, keep practicing.

Zig Ziglar, the grandfather of motivation, once said, "People often say that motivation doesn't last. Well, neither does bathing— that's why we recommend it daily." Similarly, proper mental imagery and self-talk are daily requirements. They will keep you focused and moving toward your goals. Self-talk—or your inner thinking about yourself—is the most powerful dialogue you will ever hear. What you say to yourself is the truth to your subconscious mind, and what you consider the truth shapes your beliefs and, ultimately, your actions. This is why positive affirmations are so powerful.

Recognize that your current reality is merely a product of the past and that success is a process rather than an event. This process begins with you envisioning having all of the prospects you desire, experiencing customers enjoying your presentations, and enjoying an abundance of sales as a result. As you imagine everything going your way, you will develop into the person in your perfect dream. Your life will correspond to this vision not because of providence but because you will be working hard to turn your vision into reality. By envisioning your perfect reality and practicing strategies to achieve success every day, you will improve not only your sales performance but your quality of life.

Cultivating the "It" Factor

By the time I became a division president for a production home builder, I could easily distinguish between sales associates who were controlling their lives with constructive beliefs and positive thoughts and those who were not. My vice presidents and I said the former group had the "it" factor. As a matter of fact, I would conduct all second interviews of sales associate applicants to determine whether they had "it" because whenever we hired an associate with "it," they would have superior results compared with other associates. These people believe that failure is not an option and that they control whether they will be successful or not. They have a burning desire to achieve their goals, and they don't allow their current circumstances to interfere with their ultimate success. They know they can create better circumstances. Do you have the "it" factor?

> Your own thoughts, beliefs, and actions contribute more to your success or failure than the housing market or your competitors do. Therefore, train your mind to create success-oriented thoughts.

Like me, you are empowered to create your reality. But in order to be successful, you must first define what success means to you. What do you want from life? What do you want to accomplish in your career? Do you want to outpace the market? Do you want to always outperform your competitors? You can do these things and more, regardless of housing economics. Your own thoughts, beliefs, and actions contribute more to your success or failure than the housing market or your competitors do. Therefore, train your mind to create success-oriented thoughts and those thoughts will birth beliefs that will help you achieve your heart's desires. Some scientists believe that humans use only about 10% of our brain's capacity. Think of what you could achieve if you had the ability to use 100% of your brain's capacity! Most of your brain's capacity is in the subconscious mind, which has power way beyond what most of us realize. Recognize this power and learn how to use it.

Have you ever felt as if you were on a roll and everything was going your way? Does it ever occur to you that those who have (money, power, success, happiness, health, love) only seem to get more? On the other hand, have you known people who never seem to get a break—who always seem like they have a cloud over their head? Ultimately, we tend to get more of whatever is going on in our lives, whether it is positive or negative. When you understand why this is true, you will be able to change your circumstances from being negative to mostly positive.

Your life reflects your beliefs. You shape those beliefs by interpreting what you observe every day. In other words, if you observe everything going your way, you tend to believe that everything goes your way, and you draw positive people, situations, and things toward you. If, on the other hand, you never seem to have enough (money, power, success, happiness, health, love), then you may begin to believe that you will never have enough, and you probably won't because your negative attitude will attract more negativity into your life.

"To sit back and let fate play its hand out and never influence it is not the way man was meant to operate."

—JOHN GLENN
Astronaut

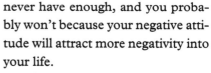

If you were guaranteed to always be successful, to have the same power as the most powerful people you can think of, and to possess the abundance of the most affluent, what would you do, change, or act upon? The awesome reality is that you already have this power of influence. You are using this power now. It is determining the outcomes of your life. So, if your present reality or circumstances are not what you desire, then you are not using it effectively. Perhaps you are not even conscious that you have this power and are using it right now.

Your thoughts create your beliefs which continually shape the person that you are. In due course, your expectations create actions and circumstances that bring about a result consistent with your thoughts every time. In other words, your outer world and your inner thoughts are one. Therefore, everything will not go your way if you are always in a bad mood. Similarly, there is no way for everything to result in failure when you're in a great mood. Your outer world will harmonize with the way you feel (or your inner world). Have you ever had a day where everything went your way? Did you feel great because everything went your way? Or, did everything go your way because you felt great? While we may tend to believe the former, the latter is the more likely explanation. The circumstances or situations that happen *to* you are really occurring *because* of you.

Take body weight. Your weight today is a result of your actions of the recent past or, perhaps, recurring behavior over a long period of time. However, if you decide today that you are going to lose weight, and you decide that failure is not an option, you already have changed your thoughts in a way to help you reach your goal of losing weight. You can act on these thoughts to change your food intake, exercise regimen, and other practices that ultimately will result in weight loss. However, if you continue to believe that you won't lose weight then you will probably not behave any differently and your weight will remain the same.

Understand that hoping for a result is different from being certain that something will happen. If you say, "I'll try to lose weight" or "I'll give it a shot," you probably won't reach your goal because you don't believe that you can. Instead, you must have certain faith in the desired result. When you decide that you will accomplish your goal to lose weight and know that nothing will prevent you from achieving it, when you expect a result as sure as the Sun rising in the morning, then you will attain it. This same principle can be applied in every aspect of your life.

You ensure success by your beliefs, which govern your behavior day to day. Tom Hopkins, a bestselling author and sales trainer urges people to, "fake it, 'til you make it."[3] In other words, every day you are creating your own reality. You are an actor in a play that you write, direct, and will review. By understanding this basic principle, you design your own reality and, therefore, determine whether you succeed or fail.

In sales, your beliefs can construct a positive outcome or destroy any possibility of success. For example, if you're selling in a community that you believe is in a less desirable part of town, you may focus on the drawbacks of the surrounding neighborhoods and then begin to believe the negative script that you have created. A prospect who visits your sales office has not ruled out the location, obviously, but you will communicate your doubts to them even if you don't realize you are doing it.

> " . . . The brain and nervous system constitute a marvelous built-in automatic guidance system which works for you as a 'success mechanism,' or against you as a 'failure mechanism,' depending on how 'YOU,' the operator operate it and the goals you set for it."[4]
>
> —DR. MAXWELL MALTZ
> *Author,* Psycho-Cybernetics

Instead, by focusing on the community's assets—its proximity to downtown offices, cultural amenities, and shopping—benefits that none of your competitors offer, you can build rapport with prospects who want the convenience that only your neighborhood has. Focusing on the benefits of your community will result in more sales.

Let's relate inconsistency between thoughts and desires to new homes sales. Attaining your sales goal will be impossible if you keep focusing on the bad market, or if you keep thinking that your sales goal is unachievable. Your negative thoughts sap your motivation to prospect for buyers or brainstorm creative solutions to low conversion rates. However, when your belief says "Yes, I can!" you will attract customers with the positive attitude and creative ideas that emanate from that belief.

Six Daily Steps

Repeat the following steps daily to create an attitude of success and ensure that you have the "it" factor:

Set goals. Define your goals, write them down, and review them daily. How much money do you desire? How many sales and closings do you need to have to achieve your financial goal? What is your timeline to achieve this goal?

Be proactive. Recognize that all circumstances start with you. You can no longer blame or credit anyone other than yourself for your current circumstances. Eliminate the "glass half empty" philosophy and always find the best in everything and everyone.

Control your thoughts. Do not allow disempowering thoughts to linger. Immediately supplant a disempowering thought with one that is empowering. If you begin to think that because the market is slow and this is not home-buying season and you probably won't sell anything this weekend, immediately change that thought. Although these negative circumstances exist, some people are still buying homes. You will meet some of these buyers, and they will purchase a home from you. Isn't that a much more empowering thought? You must believe that success is guaranteed.

Visualize success. See yourself enjoying the success you've attained by achieving the goals you've set. Visualize the home you live in, the car you drive, the clothes you wear, the awards you receive, and the loving relationships that surround you. See yourself at a company event being honored for the top sales award. See yourself at a charity auction making a significant donation to your favorite cause. See yourself at a dinner party in your new home with your new car in the driveway.

Follow a plan. Set systems in place to ensure that you do the most important things first, then be disciplined and follow them. Spend your time and money only on things that give you the desired return. For example, obtain the education you need and get the Certified New Home Sales Professional or Member of the Institute for Residential Marketing designation that you know will help you to attain your goals. Don't procrastinate. There is no better time to do it than now.

Repeat affirming words. Make daily affirmations a part of your routine and your vocabulary. Add at least 5 of your own affirmations to the following list and repeat them aloud each morning and night:

1. I love my work.
2. I am extremely efficient and get more done in less time than most people.
3. I follow through with tasks and take responsibility.
4. I own my failures and my accomplishments.
5. I make a difference.
6. It feels great when I do my job well.
7. I am passionate in my work and the money naturally follows.
8. I am grateful for my success.
9. I always work with and for wonderful people.
10. There are no limitations to what I can accomplish.
11. My thoughts control my beliefs and my beliefs create my destiny.
12. I can be what I decide to be.

Worksheet 1.1 is a tool to help you control your thoughts and beliefs (*see* Appendix). On the blank lines, write your thoughts, visions, and affirmations. Complete this form and read it daily, at least once in the morning and once in the evening. Read it just before you go to sleep so your subconscious mind can continue to focus upon these thoughts and visions all night long.

By understanding the power of positive thinking, you can supplant any negative situation with a positive one. You can have abundance instead of poverty, wisdom instead of ignorance, pleasure instead of pain, and freedom instead of oppression. You can attract anything that you desire and which you have the discipline to pursue. Be open to possibilities. Inspired thought, gut feeling, and intuition can help you discern opportunity. Then, when opportunity knocks, you must open the door.

2

The Buying and Selling Processes

Once you appreciate and begin to harness the power of your thoughts and actions in the sales process, you have the foundation on which to build a successful sales career. But before you can assist your prospect, you must align your selling process with prospects' buying process.

In fact, one of the greatest challenges sales associates *and* prospects face is buying and selling processes that are not aligned. Not surprisingly, prospects and sellers need different things. Prospects often avoid sales associates because of this disparity. The sales process often wastes the prospects' time. Therefore, if you want to sell homes, you must become a master at aligning your selling process with a prospect's buying process.

The Critical Path

In order to ensure that the transaction with prospects succeeds, we must address the following six areas often referred to as the Critical Path:

1. Greet and build rapport.
2. Qualify the customer.
3. Present the offering.
    ◆ location
    ◆ community
    ◆ home
    ◆ home site
    ◆ builder
    ◆ financing
4. Overcome resistance.
5. Close the sale.
6. Follow up with service.

However, as with any complex social interaction, the sales process does not unfold along a linear path. The stages of a sales transaction don't occur in the same order with every prospect. They may overlap and often do not occur in a single visit. Moreover, prospects are usually well into the buying process before you even meet. The circle in figure 2.1 illustrates an integrated selling process.

FIGURE 2.1 Integrated Selling Process

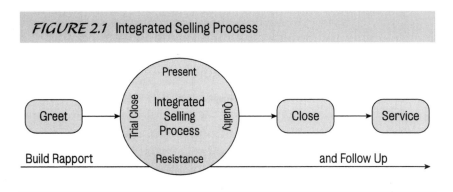

10 Stages in the Buying Process

A prospect generally follows 10 stages in the buying process (fig. 2.2), but you may not encounter that person until the fifth stage. The 10 stages are as follows:

1. Life Event
2. Awareness of Need
3. Information Search
4. First-Round Eliminations
5. Driving Frenzy
6. Evaluating Options
7. Second-Round Eliminations
8. Appraisal-Type Evaluation
9. Home Decision
10. Aftermath

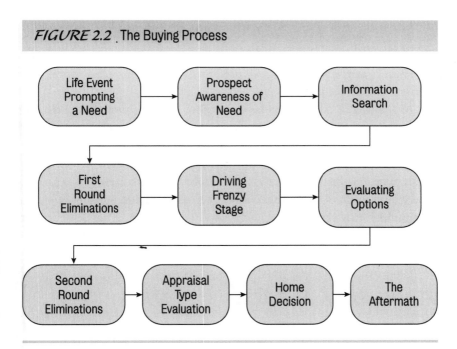

FIGURE 2.2 The Buying Process

Life Event

Understanding the life event that prompts a prospect to visit your community or model center is essential to effectively serving customers. This life event, rather than the first encounter with you, is actually the prospect's first step in the buying process. After becoming aware of how an event impacts daily living, a prospect begins to search for information about a possible home purchase, start the elimination process, and visit homes and communities.

Many life events can prompt or influence a home purchase. For example, a child moving out of the home creates two households where there was once only one. Each new household has different needs. The parents need fewer bedrooms and often desire a more urban lifestyle than what their previous neighborhood had. The child becomes a first-time home buyer. Affordability is often his or her key concern.

Conversely, when a couple marries, they combine two households into one, with new home requirements. Newlyweds may plan to remain childless, to have children immediately, or to wait and have children later. If the marriage creates a blended family, more square footage and a more family friendly environment may be needed immediately. Other families with children, or those contemplating having children, look for specific community attributes. They may prefer an outlying suburb or rural area with a good school district.

Middle-aged buyers may be looking for a larger home and have different design requirements to accommodate aging parents from what they had for their children's spaces. For example, they may want more privacy or even a separate living space for their parents. A divorce or a spouse's death often results in a desire for a smaller home because there is no one with whom to share household chores and maintenance. Job loss or a promotion also can change how and where families live. They assess their wants and needs for a home differently.

Awareness of Need

Prospects may feel the impact immediately and begin to investigate a home purchase right away, or they may not be aware of their impact until years later.

Here's an example: Your prospect has gotten a promotion. She has been able to save more money and, as her financial stability has improved, she realizes that she is living below her means. She begins to investigate a new home purchase.

Information Search

Once customers realize how their housing needs have changed, they begin gathering information to determine what will better meet their needs. They will consider location and neighborhood first, and then other issues such as the home, home site, financing, and builder. Home seekers typically consult friends, family, and various media, including the Internet, before they actually visit communities or tour properties. Thus, their minds begin to shape their vision of the perfect home even before they step inside one of your models. Before they meet you, they will have found a desired area or areas, determined their own price range, and decided what type of home will best meet their needs.

Approaching Web Site Visitors

Thanks to the Web, they can conduct much of their initial research in the comfort of their home or office, without talking to a Realtor or sales associate. In fact, more than 80% will use the Internet in the information search stage, not only to find homes and communities but to determine how much home they can afford and to get mortgage preapproval.

What does this mean to the new home sales associate? Your prospect already has some knowledge about your offering and they have already made some preliminary decisions. They have as much information or more as what you offer in your brochure. However, do not assume that this prospect has the same quality of information as a prospect that has visited your community in person. That simply is not the case, and if you assume it is, you may lose a sale. A Web site will educate your prospect, but it will not sell your offering. Furthermore, prospects will filter the education they get from a builder's Web site through their personal interests.

Therefore, do not treat online visitors as if they are returning customers. They are certainly more qualified prospects than people who are receiving information about your community for the first time: You know your Web site sparked an interest that has led them to your community. However, keep in mind that the quality of information you can provide in person and experiencing your offering "live" will be far superior to what they experienced by visiting your Web site. Consider the following three factors:

- **Information versus assistance.** A professional sales associate assists prospects through every stage of the buying decision, not just information gathering.
- **Plans versus homes.** Many people have difficulty visualizing a home from a home plan. Do not assume that what they have seen on the Web site is what they will like in reality.

◆ **Homes versus communities.** Your community is extremely difficult to present properly on the Internet. Nothing can show the prospect what life really would be like if she lived there better than visiting your neighborhood and experiencing it for herself.

If you neglect to consider these factors when talking to Web site visitors, you may proceed down a fruitless path of trying to sell them a home that ultimately is not best for them and that does not accomplish their goals.

First-Round Eliminations

Naturally, as prospects search for information, they eliminate from consideration homes and communities that don't fulfill their needs. A home or community could be within the wrong price range, school district, or commuting distance. Because they are gathering information electronically and through other means, eliminations typically begin before prospects ever get to your community. With such a high percentage of prospects using the Internet to gather information, a community may be eliminated because of its Web site or lack thereof.

If you are working with a home builder that does not have a Web site, prospects may eliminate your community simply because they could not find enough information about your offering. If you are fortunate enough even without a Web site to attract visitors or callers, they may not have enough background information about your product, builder, or community. You will need to work extra hard to provide details about your offering while you build rapport with these prospects.

Although a builder's marketing efforts play into this first round of eliminations, choosing a particular builder is usually not a high priority at this stage.

Driving Frenzy

After prospects have narrowed their choices, they begin to visit communities and homes in person, eliminating still more from consideration. They may tour 30 or more locations during this second round of eliminations. Location still factors into decisions made during the driving frenzy stage. Prospects may also consider the appearance of the community entrance, of existing home owners, and of cars in the driveways of the existing homes. Some prospects may get out of their cars and talk to existing home owners and even walk through homes under construction. When they do the latter they are likely observing the behavior of trade contractors as well as the cleanliness and finishes of the homes themselves.

Many prospects assess the appearance of the neighborhood entrance. If it doesn't pass their criteria, they may never drive in. Additionally, prospects regularly drive through neighborhoods and will eliminate them based on something they observed in the community or something they required that they didn't observe within the community. This is why your neighborhood must be in pristine condition.

As many of my associates have heard me say repeatedly, "I want it to look like Disney!" Keep the landscape and all of the common areas immaculate. Ensure there are no weeds in the plant beds and that landscaping is mulched, edged, and trimmed. The model homes and community center should look like they have just been pressure washed. Working exterior lights are essential. Visitors should not see construction debris while driving through the community. Vacant sites must be maintained and the "available" and "sold" signs should be clean and erected as appropriate.

The neighborhood should also reflect the target market. If the target market is a first-time home buyer, then the community should be designed with families in mind. It should have amenities appropriate for young children, such as a playground, pool with shallow areas, and sports field.

Welcoming Prospects

The traditional critical path to a sale that many of us learned as budding sales associates suggests that you should qualify your prospect on their first visit. Qualifying is the process of determining if the prospect is ready, willing, and able to purchase your home. Candidly, using that approach in today's environment could eliminate your home and community from the prospect's list of options. Instead, become a knowledgeable resource for buyers not only by understanding the construction process and financing but also your local community and school issues. If you hesitate to answer customers' questions on these issues they may think that you are uninformed or, even more problematic, not trustworthy. The prospect's goal is to gather information about homes and communities and then eliminate those that do not meet their needs. Therefore, at this stage, your objective is to provide prospects information and show them how your offering will fulfill their needs. If you do this correctly you will *not* be eliminated.

Follow these guidelines to align your sales process with the prospect's goals:

- **State questions so they assist the customer.** If you appear to be self-serving, your home and community may be eliminated for that reason alone.
- **Greet your prospects as soon as they arrive** at your office or model. Get out of your chair and go to the customer. Do not "curb qualify" prospects. Regardless of their appearance, treat everyone who walks into your model center as a qualified buyer until you determine otherwise.
- **Be prepared to provide logical reasons** for the prospect to own your home. Although buyers make purchasing decisions emotionally, they justify their emotional decisions logically.
- **Limit sales office time** during an initial visit to 10 to 15 minutes. If prospects give you more time, they are signaling that they like what they see. However, you must respect their time during this crucial initial visit.
- **Close the interaction** with prospects by telling them what you will do for them next and when you intend to do it. Then, do what you said you would.
- **Show them the home plan** before leading prospects on a model tour, and give them a copy of it for later reference. Make sure the home plan they get has the correct garage orientation. Some people need to see the dimensions on paper, versus seeing a room, to understand room uses.
- **Give them a take-home packet** that has a list of included home features, pricing for options displayed in the models, and home site availability. A more comprehensive packet would include a list of available inventory; information about local schools, shopping, and transportation; your builder's story; information about available financing; and any special offers available.

♦ **Add value to their time.** People don't like to work with sales people because they're afraid they'll be "sold" something they don't want. Instead, focus on their agenda first. Make sure you help them accomplish their goals during their visit efficiently and effectively.

♦ **Present your models.** If you adhere to their agenda, then you can present models without the prospect feeling pressured. This presentation will not only add value to their time, it will add value to your homes. It is crucial to your ability to develop rapport and ultimately increase your home sales.

Follow your prospects out the door and notice what they do as they leave your community. If they toss your brochure into the backseat or in the pile of other material that they have accumulated during the driving frenzy stage, then you probably have been eliminated. However, if the brochure stays in the front seat and they look at your home plans or any of the other material you provided, you probably have made the cut and the prospect will return.

Evaluating Options

During this stage of the buying process, prospects compare and evaluate the differences between offerings. They evaluate the location, community, home sites, home plans, builder, financing, and price. They assess the value of each offering.

Prospects evaluate location in relation to their preferred social activities and place of employment. They consider community amenities, how well the community is maintained, and whether people who live in the neighborhood seem similar to themselves. People like to live in neighborhoods where others share their interests and lifestyle.

Most prospects have an idea of their ideal home site size. They consider maintenance and privacy. In considering home plans, the prospect assesses whether the plan will fulfill his or her basic requirements. If even part of the plan does not, the home loses value in the prospect's eyes.

During the evaluation stage of the buying process, buyers consider the builder's reputation, the amount of control that the builder will allow the prospect to maintain, and the expected delivery date of the home. They also consider financing incentives, convenience, and flexibility.

The prospect weighs all of these considerations against the base price, and the prospect's assessment of the value of each offering becomes the basis for the next round of eliminations.

Second Round Eliminations

In the second round of eliminations, most home seekers will narrow their choices to no more than five communities. During this phase, prospects may or may not enter your model center. If they do, you generally can assume that your neighborhood has passed their various tests. Now they will be trying to find the right builder. Greet and treat them professionally during their visit. They are important, and they want to be treated accordingly. They want you to provide information about your homes and community. If you don't, they may eliminate your community from consideration.

The sales associate's objective during the prospect's first visit must be to add value to the prospect's time. Prospects want to be asked about their needs; they do not want to be asked self-serving questions. For example, sales associates often ask the prospect, "Is this your first visit?" Prospects quickly learn that a sales associate asks this question to determine whether he or she has a financial interest in the customer. If the prospect had visited before but worked with a different sales associate, then the sales associate often will not be interested in helping the prospect because there is less financial incentive for them to do so. If the prospect is visiting for the first time, then the sales associate may be more motivated to assist the prospect in hopes of earning a commission.

Prospects have figured out that if they say it is their first visit to a neighborhood, then the sales associate will pay attention to them. If they are a returning customer and the sales associate they dealt with previously is not there, then they are likely to be left alone. Instead of asking self-serving questions, focus on the prospect's needs and strive to fulfill them.

The sales associate must provide, at a minimum, the following information during a prospect's first visit:

- ◆ home plans
- ◆ neighborhood layout
- ◆ included features
- ◆ list of inventory

- information on special promotions
- financing information
- background on the home building company

Prospects aren't interested in conversing with sales associates unless the conversation is directly related to the information they want. Their objective on the first visit is to gather information, not to have to provide information to you. Start your relationship by adding value to their time, and you will eventually be able to transition to a more assertive sales approach.

Details Matter

A prospect may eliminate your community without ever seeing your model center or home plans. To ensure maximum foot traffic in your sales office, your community must look immaculate. You are responsible for ensuring that your builder is aware of the problems he or she must correct to ensure that prospects don't just drive by your community. If you don't present yourself, the product, the community, the location, and the builder in the best possible light, you can quickly be eliminated from consideration by home seekers.

Drive-by appeal is crucial. A clean neighborhood and model center tell your buyers you build quality homes. To improve a builder's chances of surviving a prospect's final elimination round, work with the construction superintendent to ensure that your neighborhoods and model center(s) are in pristine condition as follows:

Community entrances and other common areas must be well groomed and landscaped. Shrubs and trees should be trimmed neatly. Flower beds should be mulched generously after removing all weeds. Walls and gates must be so clean that they look freshly painted.

Construction sites must be clean. Trash on the jobsite communicates a lack of quality and attention to detail to potential buyers. Therefore, the builder must have a policy for cleanliness on jobsites, and the sales associate must be the watchdog to ensure that trade contractors and other workers comply with it.

The streetscape should include a variety of elevations so prospects can see how they can customize their home.

When prospects drive through the community and see that the builder has taken care of every detail, they will know that you and your company deliver a quality product.

Move-in-Ready Models

Prospects see the model home as an indicator of the quality of all of a builder's homes. They believe—and rightly so—that what they observe in the model is what they will have in their new home. Ensure that your model homes are maintained as follows:

◆ **The model center landscape must be as pristine** as your entryways with grass mowed and edged and flower beds and trees maintained. Model home exteriors must be free of mud daubers, wasp nests, spiderwebs, and anything else that keeps the home from looking move-in ready.

◆ **The interior of the models must be clean** and merchandised appropriately to the target market. For example, if you are selling affordable homes, don't go overboard staging the models with lavish accessories that buyers won't relate to because they can't afford these furnishings.

◆ **All lights must work.** If you don't care enough to replace a burnt-out lightbulb, what else don't you care about that prospects *don't* see?

◆ **Interior finishings must work properly.** Cabinet doors close correctly, doors align, doors and second-story floors don't squeak, molding is mitered perfectly, and anything else a buyer can see or hear has received proper attention from the builder's crews.

Consider staging a model with only included features, or with very few options, such as upgraded flooring and cabinets if you have multiple models. Customers have difficulty understanding how an upgraded home would look without the optional items.

Appraisal-Type Evaluation

During their final evaluation and elimination process, prospects will visit the model center, their desired home, and preferred home site several times. They will compare included features, home plans, optional features, home sites, financing, and the benefits of the builder. They will assess the quality of both the builder and the homes in a process similar to car buying, in which the manufacturer plays a key role in the buyer's decision and the perception of quality.

Therefore, consider that before the prospect's second or subsequent visits to your community, they have shopped around. They probably are considering both new homes and resales. They have a better understanding of the types of homes that are available to them and how much money they will need to invest in owning a home. They are more educated than when they first visited your community and probably have fine-tuned their home preferences or their preferences may have changed completely since their first visit.

At this stage, prospects place value and quality above price and image. In fact, consumer surveys indicate that the former two factors are three times more important than the latter two. Don't confuse appearance and image, though. Appearances actually shape the consumer's perception of quality—either positively or negatively. Prospects assess the fit and finish of model home features, cleanliness of the neighborhood and jobsites, and attractiveness of streetscapes. With few exceptions, construction details, such as R-values of insulation, are not critical factors for prospects during this stage of their evaluation.

Most prospects are seeking logical reasons to keep your home on their list of viable options. As a sales associate, you must provide them with these reasons by thoroughly understanding the tradeoffs inherent in any home purchase and, in particular, for all of the options your specific prospects are considering.

For example, a prospect may prefer the amenities your community offers but another builder's home design. You must artfully show the prospect how your community's amenities will provide quality-of-life benefits far beyond what the other builder's home design would.

Home Decision

In the final stage before making a home purchase decision, prospects narrow their options further and weigh each and every factor, including the home, home site, community, location, builder, included features, and financing. They will use logic to justify their emotional home purchase decision. At this stage, the sales associate who has fostered the best relationship and/or the strongest ability to justify the value of their offering often is the winner. That's because a strong relationship with customers allows you to influence their decisions because you thoroughly understand their dominant buying motives. You know which areas they are willing to compromise on and which they aren't. Listen to the prospects, communicate to them that what they want is important to you, and make them feel comfortable that purchasing from your builder would be a wise decision. Never forget that buying a home is not only a significant financial investment but probably the most emotional buying decision most of us will ever make.

In the 1990s when I was Vice President of Sales and Marketing for Centex Homes, their sales training program introduced the concept that price, value, and image were the three major influencers in a prospect's buying decision. Figure 2.3 shows the relative importance of specific areas that influence these three factors. It is based on my professional experience working with prospects.

Aftermath

Your job doesn't end with a home purchase because everyone buyers talk to after they leave your sales office will cause them to second-guess their decision. Buyer's remorse will set in. You need to anchor the buyer's decisions with the help of the design center consultant, superintendent, and loan officer. Everyone who has contact with the future home owner must ensure that the customer still feels good about their decision throughout the construction and options selection process, final walk-through, at the closing table, through the warranty period, and beyond.

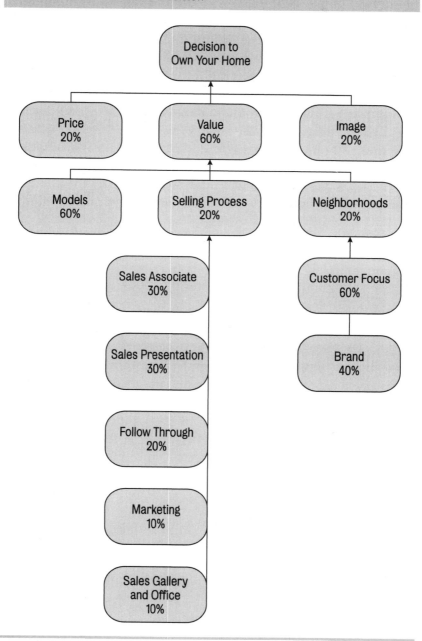

FIGURE 2.3 Relative Importance of Factors Influencing a Home Purchase Decision

3

Prospecting Skills and Follow-up

*M*any new home sales professionals think the builder is responsible for prospecting. However, professional sales associates understand that they can take specific actions to create additional prospects and by doing so they can boost their sales results. Therefore, throw out your limiting, preconceived notions of what your builder should do for you and creatively brainstorm what you can do for your builder. Consider the following grassroots efforts to improve the quality and quantity of your prospects.

Targeted marketing often works better than blind direct mail campaigns. Consider everyone who needs a home in your price range and reach out to them through their likely affiliations, such as the following:

Neighborhoods. Most people move to homes that are close to where they are living. Therefore, apartment complexes and communities with homes priced lower than yours are ideal sources of prospects. Doorknob hangers can proclaim, "Own for less than rent!" If a broker manages any of the communities, you might consider a cooperative arrangement with them to encourage them to refer people to your community. If you are selling homes in an age-restricted community, look for prospects in nearby neighborhoods of single-family homes. In addition, consider direct mail or even teaming with a community manager to offer incentives to residents. You should at least contact people (or their Realtors) who have their homes on the market because they may be looking for new homes.

Remember that prior to selling new homes, I worked in the banking industry. I made cold calls selling an unsecured debt program. This program was not popular in the savings industry. Given the tough selling situation, I had to use my creativity. By the time I entered new home sales, I was used to prospecting differently from other sales associates.

With that background and as a novice in the new home sales industry in the early 1990s, I had the opportunity to work at a condominium community. The units had 891 sq. ft. of living space, 2 bedrooms, and 2 baths. There was no covered parking. But at the time, they were more spacious than most apartments nearby. The units were priced at $69,990. My prospecting strategy was as follows: I hired 2 teenagers in the neighborhood for $10 each to go door-to-door with a flyer I designed that offered renters the opportunity to "Own for Less than Rent." The teens distributed these to the doors of the apartments after noon on Sundays when the leasing offices had closed. They also placed the flyers on vehicle windshields in a nearby shopping plaza.

I am not suggesting that you violate "No Soliciting" regulations, only that you think creatively. This $20 investment each weekend usually resulted in 5 to 8 additional prospects per week and about 1 additional sale per week for the few weeks the flyer campaign occurred. Others in the company could not understand why I was selling so many homes in a community where no more than 2 units per month had sold during the previous several months.

Military bases, universities, and major employers. All of these institutions have a department or staff that is responsible for helping with off-base, off-campus, or relocation housing. Introduce yourself to these individuals so they will think of your community first when assisting people with a home search. They are usually very happy to work with you.

My associates and I have had great success following this advice. For example, $1 move-in programs work beautifully in any market where Veterans Administration (VA) loans are popular. Also, hospital employees can be great prospects. Facing shortages of nurses and doctors, many hospitals offer relocation benefits. Contact their human resources departments. Consider every large employer in your area and ask yourself how your community would benefit their employees. If appropriate, contact the companies' relocation or human resources departments to determine how you can work together to offer a benefit to their employees that will lead to home sales in your community.

Real estate brokers. Brokers often represent 50 to 70% of a builder's business, and these relationships require an investment from you as well as from the home building company owners. Consider the following strategies for increasing your Realtor business:

- Host breakfast or lunch at your community.
- Make presentations during brokerage office sales meetings.
- Leave cookies, candy, and information about your communities at brokerage offices.
- Offer open houses for Realtors at your community with brochures and incentives.
- Visit open houses in nearby communities that may feed new prospects to your community.
- List inventory on the multiple listing service and put lock boxes on your homes.
- Allow phone registrations and extended registration periods.

Incentives

Do you allow home-to-sell contingencies? Many prospects today would like to move into a larger or smaller home, or change geographic areas, but first they must sell their current homes. Moving forward with your home but allowing the customer to cancel without forfeiting their deposit if their current home does not sell broadens the number of prospects that can buy your new homes and provides opportunities to reward your best Realtors. Prospects who have not yet listed their homes for sale often will look to you for Realtor suggestions. Provide these leads to your top producers who are listing agents. You will foster loyalty among these Realtors and sell more homes.

Bonuses

Some builders offer bonuses to Realtors. However, news about these programs generally travels slowly because Realtors are bombarded with information about opportunities for their clients. They tend to recall or focus only on those opportunities relevant to their current clients. Therefore, broker bonuses on inventory often do not work well unless they are offered on all inventory for at least three months. Your broker programs should be long-term—in effect for at least six months, if not longer. Ideally, your company's broker incentive program applies to every community and rewards Realtors who sell more than one home for your company. In communicating with Realtors about the program, use a multifaceted awareness strategy, which will increase the likelihood that Realtors will remember your community. To spread the word about a program or incentive, you can contact Realtors by sending flyers to realty offices, e-mailing them, advertising in their newsletters, or visiting their meetings.

As in any business, you can compensate your top producers with the best pay. Keep a VIP list of Realtors and pay them in proportion to their loyalty. Of course, you need to provide good reasons for these Realtors to sell your homes rather than your competitors'.

Internet Prospecting

Does your builder have a Web site? It is an essential prospecting tool and is a minimum Internet marketing requirement today. Make no mistake, a Web site is not a selling tool but a prospecting tool. If a prospect cannot buy your home on the Internet without human intervention, then your builder should not attempt to sell your homes on the Internet. The objective of an effective Web site is developing prospects. The goal is to prompt the Web site visitor to come to your community in person.

As previously discussed, in the information gathering stage of the buying process prospects find reasons to eliminate offerings that do not meet their requirements. Your Web site should ensure that you are not eliminated, which means you must include information on your homes, home sites, community, location, builder, and financing so the prospect can determine if you are likely to have what will fulfill their needs.

Many in the industry view a builder's Web site generally as an opportunity to present a virtual brochure with home plans, neighborhood layout, area map, builder story, and special financing. Although some Web sites present included features as well, I see no need to present them on the Web site. Included features are irrelevant if the prospect is not interested in the rest of your offering. In addition, you may give the prospect a reason *not* to visit in person.

What Users Want

The three most important considerations in designing your Web site are that it loads quickly, is user-friendly, and provides the ability to request more information. Although high-resolution graphics look appealing, they can make a Web page slow to load, so balance graphics and speed in your Web site design.

The second factor, user-friendliness, means ease of navigating your site. Many prospects want to view home plans first. Being able to view plans easily before visiting your neighborhoods will simplify prospects' home search process. Make sure your home plans, elevations, neighborhood layouts, area map, and other elements will print for the user as large as in your brochures. Ultimately, you want your Web site to be an enhanced brochure prospects can access within seconds instead of having to wait to receive materials by mail.

Third, you want the prospect to be able to request more information easily. Therefore, only require them to provide a name and e-mail address rather than asking them to complete a survey. Allow telephone numbers and e-mail addresses to be optional to alleviate users' fears about having salespeople contact them. If you require telephone numbers and e-mail addresses, you may preclude some prospects from contacting you.

Effective Follow-up

Attracting a prospect is only the first step in a multifaceted sales process in which you will demonstrate not only your model homes and community but also your excellent follow-up and communication skills.

Internet Inquiries

When you receive an inquiry from your builder's Web site, you should respond within minutes during business hours. If a prospect provides their e-mail address and telephone number, they are giving you permission to use them. Assuming that your Web site provides most or all of the information in your brochure, you must have additional information to provide when you contact prospects who visited your Web site.

A telephone call to the prospect can start as follows:

> "Hello, Ms. Robinson. My name is Tammy with Creation Communities. I just received your Internet request for more information about our community. Most of the information in our community brochure is already on our Web site, so I wanted to inquire if there was something specific you were looking for."

In addition to providing the desired information, the telephone call is a perfect opportunity to inquire about when the prospect plans to visit as well as what prompted her to inquire about obtaining additional information.

If you have an e-mail address for a prospect, but not a telephone number, you can use a similar script in your e-mail response.

Community Visitors

Only about 5% of prospects will commit to buying a home on their first visit to your model center. The other 95% probably will look at other new homes and builders, as well as resales, as part of their appraisal and narrowing process. Therefore, you will need to learn strategies and follow practices that will encourage visitors to return to your community. Attracting repeat visits among your prospects will increase your company's return on its marketing investment and help you to have long-term success in sales. Communicate regularly and systematically with prospects. Your goal is not necessarily to have them return immediately. Many of us were taught that a good sales associate should follow up with prospects to close on an appointment to visit or revisit your community and that anything short of that achievement was considered failure. Although it is true that prospects must return in order to purchase a home, if a return visit is your only goal you probably will feel like a failure if they don't come back. The losing scenario then will become a self-fulfilling prophesy. Instead, the goal of your follow-up calls should be to assess the quality of each prospect so you can craft an effective follow-up strategy. If you do this, your follow-up calls will always be successful.

Begin by asking yourself, "If I received three phone calls within four weeks and the subject of those calls interested me, would I return at least one of the calls?" The odds are that you would. On the other hand, if you were not interested in the subject of the calls, would you return the call? You probably would not. The good news is that with or without a return call a sales associate can assess the quality of the prospect. The primary purpose of following up with prospects is to give adequate attention to all of them based upon their sense of urgency, willingness, and ability to purchase your home.

Prospects are more likely to return your calls if you ask their permission to be contacted before they leave your community. You can request permission as follows: "Susan, as you know, the market seems to be always changing. If there's something that occurs that might affect your new home decision, would you like me to contact you about it?" If she says yes, then ask, "What's the best way to reach you?" You have prepared Susan for your call, so she is likely to answer it.

Rating Prospects and Executing Your Follow-up

To maximize returns on the time you spend making follow-up calls, consider using the following rating system to categorize your prospects:

A. The prospect is ready, willing, and able to buy a home, and your homes seem to be consistent with what they want. Once they find the right home, they can move forward.

B. The prospect does not have one of the three requirements. They are not ready, not willing, or not able to buy. However, your homes seem consistent with what they want. Once all of the three requirements are fulfilled, the prospect can move forward with a purchase.

C. The prospect is missing two of the three requirements but what you have to offer seems consistent with what they desire.

D. You would rate this prospect as an A, B, or C; however, they don't want what you have to offer.

E. This prospect isn't looking for a home but might know someone now or in the future who might be interested buying one.

Most medium- to large-volume builders have a database management system that sales associates can use to manage prospects. This system is often integrated into the sales order processing, accounting, and purchasing systems. However, many of these systems do not include the tools needed in an effective prospect management system. Smaller builders may not have any system for sales at all.

In any regard, you are responsible for following up with your prospects and managing that process. Even if you must purchase an off-the-shelf database management software program on your own, you want to ensure that whatever system you use includes the ability to

- merge address information into letters
- merge e-mail address information into e-mail messages
- schedule letters, e-mails, and phone call reminders automatically according to the rating you have assigned to the prospect
- generate reports that allow you to understand where your prospects are coming from

You should make the first follow-up call to prospects who rate A to D on the day of their first visit. In fact, if possible, it should be completed immediately after prospects leave your sales office. Yes, that's correct. This first message is better left as voice mail, but because it is a feel-good call, you can still deliver it if the prospect answers the phone. Simply thank them sincerely for their time because not many of us have any time to spare today. The call will remind them of your community. You also can take the opportunity to prepare prospects for your next planned follow-up call. You can customize the following script to suit your situation:

> "Good afternoon, Susan. This is Tammy with Creation Communities at Oak Trace. I know you just left my community, but I wanted to call to simply thank you for your time. I plan on touching base with you no later than Saturday after I've gathered the information you requested. If you need to speak with me prior to that time, feel free to give me a buzz at (000) 123-4567. Thanks again for your time, Susan, and have an awesome week."

Adding Value

Most prospects who don't like to deal with salespeople feel that way because they don't think their agendas are compatible and, therefore, they view the interaction as a waste of time. Therefore, reiterate that you want to add value to their time, not waste it, and then follow through with that promise. This assurance will help prospects feel better about accepting future calls from you.

For future calls, just introduce yourself, your company, and your community, and then mention a unique feature of your community that will jog the prospect's memory. After you are certain that she remembers you, you no longer have to mention this community attribute. Here's an example:

> "Hello, Susan, this is Tammy from Creation Communities at Oak Trace. We're the neighborhood off of Thirty-eighth Avenue in Bradenton that has all of the established oak trees."

After the prospect recognizes you, immediately set a time limit for the call. Setting limits is critical if you want the prospect to allow you to continue. For example, you could say, "Susan, it will take me about two minutes to explain why I'm calling. Is now a good time to talk?" After the prospect agrees to talk, explain why you are calling. The four most common purposes are to

- provide information she requested
- provide information you were unable to share during her visit
- apologize for not having been able to spend more time with her, if appropriate
- share something that requires the prospect to return to the community

Typically, you can assess the prospect's interest, or lack thereof, by her phone manner or tone of voice. If you have information that requires the prospect to return to the community and the prospect indicates she is interested in doing so, you may invite her to return. However, if you invite her to return even if she does not seem interested in doing so, she will probably reject future follow-up calls. The following are good reasons for a return visit:

- new incentive
- plan redesign
- new financing program
- release of additional home sites
- new inventory home coming on the market
- brand-new plan

Managing Prospects

After the first follow-up call on the day of the prospect's first visit, the timing of additional follow-up calls depends on prospects and their urgency to find a new home. There are many ways to manage your prospects; however, you should use a contact management software program to ensure that you're efficient, as I previously mentioned. If your company doesn't provide this software, I recommend you acquire it on your own. Using the ratings system, here is how you should proceed with follow-up calls:

A prospects. A prospects simply need to find what suits their needs and then they will be able to move forward. These prospects require immediate follow-up and, depending on their personalities, are likely to return phone calls and ask questions. In addition to placing the first follow-up call immediately after they leave your office, also plan to call them again no later than 48 hours after their visit. Whether or not you can fulfill their needs will determine whether you make future calls, but as long as they are A prospects you should communicate with them at least weekly.

Telephone calls and e-mail are the preferred communication methods for A prospects because of the time lag with traditional mail. Telephone is always the preferred method of communication if you need information from them in order to move toward closing.

B prospects. You should follow up with B prospects within a week of their initial visit. The objective with B prospects is not only to find a home to suit them but to move them to become A prospects. You may contact B prospects every two to four weeks depending upon their specific situation. Use telephone and e-mail to communicate with B prospects for the same reasons you use these methods with A prospects.

C prospects. C prospects should also get their first follow-up call within a week of their initial visit. Additional follow-up calls should occur at least quarterly until they become an A or B prospect. Many times the goal in contacting C prospects is to update them about something new. If they don't need to respond to a specific issue, use e-mail or even traditional mail service to communicate with them.

Communicating with Impact

In addition to telephoning your prospects, you can e-mail them and even send them regular mail. When using e-mail, reintroduce yourself, your builder, and your community as you would on the phone. For greater impact, you may include photos of the neighborhood, a new home plan, information about inventory, or anything new about the area that would generate interest. Because some people respond better to pictures and others to words, strive to incorporate both in your e-mail communication.

Although e-mail has replaced most postal mail, some prospects will be late adopters of technology and you will need to communicate with them by snail mail. If you use snail mail, handwrite the envelope to decrease the chances of it being discarded.

Responding to Prospects' Requests

With few exceptions, when responding to prospects' requests, you should communicate using the same method they used to make their request. If you receive a letter, respond with a letter. If they call you, call them back. If they e-mail you, respond accordingly.

However, if a prospect's e-mail or Web site inquiry provides a telephone number even though it was not requested or required, you can presume that you may call. The same holds true for guest registrations. If the prospect provides a telephone number, then he or she is giving permission to call. You also may want to alter the communication method if you need information from the prospect in order to answer a question. For example, you may want to respond to an e-mail message by phone instead of e-mailing back and forth.

When communicating in writing, do so carefully: Avoid spelling errors and grammatical mistakes, and keep sentences and paragraphs short. Also, keep in mind that the recipient cannot see your body language or hear your vocal inflection in written communication. Therefore, choose your words, phrases, and punctuation carefully.

Although electronic slang has crept into e-mail, don't treat e-mail messages as informal communications. E-mail is not the appropriate venue for "chat lingo." The impression you leave with prospects begins with your first communication. Keep your messages professional and on-task and use a signature that identifies you and your company. If you need a response to your e-mail, indicate that in the subject line. For example, the subject line for a message to a prospect who requests more information through your Web site may be "Information Needed to Respond to your Creation Communities Inquiry."

Most home decisions don't occur on the first visit, yet most sales associates find it difficult to follow up with prospects effectively. By implementing the preceding ideas in your follow-up routine, you will feel more comfortable staying in touch with your prospects, and you will boost return visits and increase sales.

E-mail Etiquette

Think twice about the content of your message before you send or reply to an e-mail. These are words you cannot take back, and they can easily be forwarded to others. Do not express anything in an e-mail you would be uncomfortable having your boss read aloud to your peers. Understand that e-mail is not private. It goes through many networks before reaching the recipient. Even after you delete a message and delete it from your deleted files, a record of it probably still exists on your company server as well as on other networks used to deliver the message to the recipient.

Be considerate of those who e-mail you. Use an "out of office" response when you are gone for more than 24 hours. Ideally, another sales associate handles new Web site inquiries while you are away, and that person responds quickly. However, your backlog of prospects and current and future home owners who e-mail you will not understand why your responses are delayed if they don't know you are away.

Do not embed graphics other than your company logo into e-mail unless recipients are on a mailing list they subscribed to. Instead, you may attach files and tell the recipient what the attachments are in your e-mail message. When sending more than two attachments, zip them into one file, which allows the recipient to download the files more efficiently and ensures that all files are downloaded.

Do not send large files unsolicited. Instead, save these files on the Internet and simply send the recipient a link to the file. If this option is not available at your company, several free hosting services are available. If you are sending an e-mail message to multiple recipients, use your own e-mail address in the "To" field and use the "BCC" field to maintain recipients' privacy.

Another important aspect of e-mail communication is ensuring that you do not infect another person's computer with a virus. Make sure you have and use antivirus software. Also, don't request a Read Notification Receipt. Many people consider it an invasion of privacy.

Most important, reply to every e-mail addressed to you. The sender is likely to be waiting for your reply even if it is just to notify them that you have received the e-mail and to thank them for the communication.

How the Critical Path Really Works

The 10-step critical path is merely a guideline for fulfilling all of your prospect's needs. Far from being rigid, the professional approach to selling is flexible.

The professional salesperson understands and has the discretion to introduce each step of the process appropriately, according to the customer's needs. This is good news because today most consumers won't allow you to qualify them until they have found something of interest. Although you must determine at some point whether they are ready, willing, and able to purchase your home, you don't need to qualify them immediately. With some customers, you may be presenting your models prior to ever asking a qualifying question. With others, you may be able to begin the qualifying process earlier in their visit. As you become more familiar with the concepts and more adept at the practices recommended in *Think Sold!*, you will be able to follow prospects' buying processes even as you identify quickly what you need to know about them, their lifestyle, and their timelines for making a home purchase. This ability to identify these details will expedite the process for both of you, resulting in increased sales and improved customer satisfaction.

Greet and Build Rapport

Many sales professionals consider greeting and building rapport with customers the most critical stage of the selling process. That's because how you handle this opening stage either earns you the right to begin selling your product's benefits or drives the customer away. You must greet prospects as soon as they arrive. After that, how you build rapport with prospects will be as unique as the customers themselves. Depending on your personality and your customer's, you may establish rapport nearly instantaneously or rapport building may take several meetings and conversations. In any case, the professional salesperson continually works at building rapport with the customer throughout the relationship. Chapters 4 and 5 discuss rapport-building strategies.

Qualify the Customer

Today, most consumers qualify themselves financially prior to their home search. Therefore, when they visit your community, they may already know their price point. If your product is an affordable home appealing to first-time home buyers, then price is paramount. First-time home buyers will need information on affordability and may ask for it on their first visit. You should be able to qualify them early in the sales process. Chapter 11 discusses financing in more detail.

Finances are not the only issue in qualifying a prospect. While customers may be financially able to purchase on paper, they also must be ready and willing to purchase in reality. Building rapport with customers can help you increase their willingness and readiness to purchase, but asking qualifying questions before attending to the relationship can be a turnoff to prospects.

Present the Offering

In order for your prospects to be able to adequately assess their options, you must provide information about your offering. How you present your product's benefits can well determine whether or not you survive a prospect's second round of eliminations. The professional sales associate will be able to demonstrate the product effectively because he or she already has developed rapport with the prospect. A sound product presentation discusses and demonstrates the location, community, homes and home sites, builder's story, and financing options. During the presentation, continue to build rapport and ask qualifying questions. By doing so, you can discover and overcome buyer resistance and ultimately close the sale. Chapter 7 discusses how to strengthen your presentation skills and make your demonstrations memorable.

Overcome Resistance

Handling resistance in a way that will work both for your benefit and for the customer's is an art. Successful sales professionals understand that negative customer feedback offers an opportunity to better understand what a customer wants and needs. For example, if prospects tell you the secondary bedrooms are too small, ask them what requirements they have for the bedrooms. You may be able to provide another home design, alter the existing one, or demonstrate how the existing bedrooms would actually meet their requirements. You can learn to skillfully handle customer objections by following the advice in chapter 9.

Close the Sale

Masterful closers are compensated for their skill at levels far above average sales associates. Therefore, top sales associates have learned the art of closing. Closing requires the sales professional to ask questions that require the customer to make decisions. Indeed, closing occurs throughout the sales process as you persuade the customer to allow you to demonstrate a home or gain agreement on a home site, for example. You are simply asking questions that require your prospect to make decisions. Closing is natural and instinctive to professional sales associates who know how to greet a customer, build rapport, and demonstrate a product.

As you build rapport with your customers and present your products, continually ask yourself what to close on next. Having closing goals throughout the sales process will help you streamline the process, guide your prospect step-by-step, and move prospects to purchase a home. Chapter 10 explains how to close with confidence.

Post-Sale Service

Post-sale service is as important as other stages in the selling process. Professional sales associates continue to deliver customer service long after they convert prospects to buyers. Excellent customer service significantly improves your overall sales success as well as the builder's customer satisfaction ratings and referrals. The sales associate is the liaison between the customer and builder.

Because the sales associate shapes customer expectations throughout the selling process, he or she is the best person to continuously communicate those expectations to others in the company. Communicate with the buyers no less than biweekly and whenever they have a deadline approaching, such as making color, option, or finish selections. Also remind them when their financing approval is due. Other contacts can simply update them on the status of their home.

After they close on the home, continue to follow up with your buyers to discuss whether the builder and home have met their expectations. Don't forget to ask for referrals, which are the lifeblood of a home building company's business! If the customer says the home, builder, or buying process did not meet their expectations, communicate this response to the builder and then follow up to determine whether the builder addressed the problem. Excellent follow-up distinguishes outstanding builders from average ones.

4

Working with
Diverse Buyers

veryone knows the golden rule of reciprocity: Treat other people as we wish to be treated. Each individual shares undeniable, inherent rights because they are human. At the same time, we are diverse—male or female, of different colors, from various national origins, with different gifts, of different sexual orientations, with many shapes and sizes, with religious traditions or none, speaking many languages, and from many cultures. But everyone should agree that all people are created equal and enjoy basic human rights. Remember this tenet when you are working with customers. Also remember that because customers are individuals, they don't all want the same thing. In other words, you must "do unto others as they wish to be done to."

The first step in understanding others' motivations so you can individualize your sales presentations is to understand the roots of your own behaviors and how you interact with others. Socrates said, "Know thyself." Indeed, your ability to understand and appreciate others depends directly on your own awareness of your habits, morals, temperament, and ability to control anger. Your perception of other people and of circumstances is distorted by your own needs and emotions. In other words, your reality is not the same as anyone else's.

You must see others as they really are instead of who you think they are. Moreover, you must see yourself as you really are and not as you think others see you. This clarity will significantly improve your communication and relationships with others. Your self-awareness will allow you to recognize whether or not your actions and behaviors are aligning well with a prospect's expectations or desires.

"The ability to get along with people is as purchasable a commodity as coffee or sugar, and I will pay more for that ability than any other on the face of the earth."

—JOHN D. ROCKEFELLER
Industrialist and Philanthropist

The ability to harmonize with and then influence others is considered the greatest asset of a sales associate. In fact, the most highly compensated sales associates have mastered the art of influence. They understand people's motivations, and they sell the way that people like to buy. Would you agree that if you understood people's motivations, your results in sales would improve significantly? If you answered yes, I have great news for you: There are a variety of tools you can use to help you understand behavior patterns. Although each person is as individual as his fingerprint and nobody fits a single profile to a tee, you can understand people better by knowing the common personality types and understanding dominant senses and learning styles.

Working with Common Personality Types

The DiSC Personal Profile and Charles J. Clarke III's Bulls, Owls, Lambs, and Tigers (the BOLT system) social style grids are two helpful tools to understand behaviors. Most social style grids recognize four primary personal styles. For example, the social style grid (fig. 4.1) shows how the four dominant personality profiles manifest responsiveness and assertiveness. The third dimension of versatility is shown in figure 4.2. Versatility—the ability to move into another's world—is a key characteristic of top sales professionals.

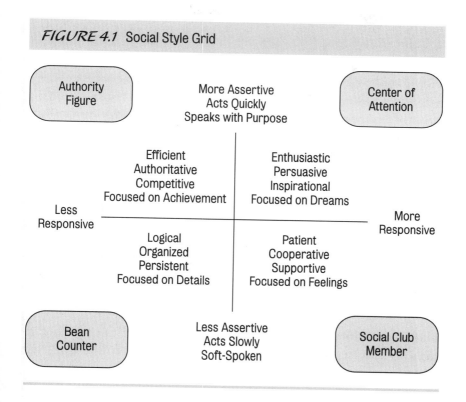

FIGURE 4.1 Social Style Grid

Authority Figure

More Assertive
Acts Quickly
Speaks with Purpose

Center of Attention

Efficient
Authoritative
Competitive
Focused on Achievement

Enthusiastic
Persuasive
Inspirational
Focused on Dreams

Less Responsive

More Responsive

Logical
Organized
Persistent
Focused on Details

Patient
Cooperative
Supportive
Focused on Feelings

Bean Counter

Less Assertive
Acts Slowly
Soft-Spoken

Social Club Member

The following are brief descriptions of common personality styles and suggestions for working effectively with them as a new home sales associate.

Authority Figure

Authority figures are like dominant bulls. Because winning is everything for them, they focus single-mindedly on their goals. Even if they are not competing with others, they are competing with themselves. They are action oriented and typically have a short attention span. Therefore, they appear impatient if you are not attending to their immediate interests. Typically, authority figures are visual or auditory communicators.

An authority figure is easy to spot because they are typically blunt and focused on their own needs. People who don't understand how the authority figure thinks may find them rude. You won't necessarily recognize them by their outward appearance, however. Because they are more focused on their own needs than on what others think about them, they

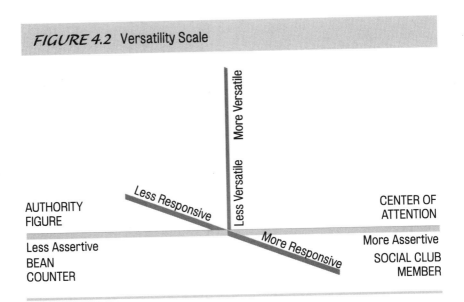

FIGURE 4.2 Versatility Scale

may not seek out typical status symbols. They are as likely to be seen driving a no-frills Jeep as a Mercedes and are as likely to wear Wrangler jeans as a Fioravanti suit.

You can appeal to authority figures by allowing them to believe they are in control, but you still must approach and respond to them with confidence. They will view giving in as a sign of weakness. Authority figures will make quick and determined decisions. Because they often can't admit they're wrong, you must present options in ways that allow them to save face if they need to change their mind. Be direct with authority figures but remain cool. Stick to the point and don't be afraid to ask for the sale. Authority figures want bottom-line results. They want you to handle the details.

Because authority figures often lack the versatility of some other personality types, they can be difficult for many people to work with. Understand and practice working effectively with them and you will avoid the frustration of other sales consultants and dramatically improve your results with authority figures.

Imagine having sales associates who are authority figures. They would have some challenges, don't you think? They're exceptional closers but struggle with building rapport. How do I know? I am an off-the-chart authority figure. I am fortunate, though, to have a higher level of versatility. Nevertheless, it became clear early in my sales career that handling resistance and closing were my strengths but building rapport and demonstrations were a struggle. Today, however, most people who see me in a sales environment would guess that my dominant style is center of attention, as discussed in the next section. The difference is not because my personality has changed; I have just learned to modify my behavior to be able to communicate more effectively with different personalities.

Center of Attention

You can recognize centers of attention by their smiles and positive energy. They are the classic extroverts who love to talk. These natural optimists are often the life of a party. They inspire others with their enthusiasm so they are naturally persuasive. These playful individuals choose their clothes and cars to be noticed. As they are visual learners, your most effective sales tool with them is usually a completed home of their plan preference.

Center of attention personality types are oriented toward feelings, emotions, and imagination. Therefore, they must feel good about their decisions in order to be excited by them. You can appeal to the center of attention personality types by complimenting them, but you also must be enthusiastic about what you are selling. Allow some flexibility in presenting to centers of attention because they will need to take short breaks from the business at hand to socialize with you. In addition to showing them a completed home, photographs, and/or illustrations, inspire centers of attention with language that will help them dream and imagine the home.

Centers of attention are assertive but because they respond to positive attention they will be open to you. However, keep in mind that these individuals are particularly prone to experiencing buyer's remorse. Because they are impulsive, they may buy before they're ready. But if what you have to offer fulfills their needs and desires, they are easy to influence as they are open and versatile in their approach to life and decision making.

Be careful if you and your prospect both are centers of attention. You may become great friends but not get any work done. Make sure you stay focused on your objective of selling her the right home.

Social Club Member

This personality type is the most common profile, and therefore you will likely have more social club member prospects than any other customer profile. Social club members place primary importance on a sense of belonging. They focus on other people's feelings, especially their family members'. Patient and cooperative, social club members provide a good support system for loved ones and do not intentionally harm others. Social club members are risk averse and don't tolerate conflict well. They prefer harmonious and predictable situations.

You can readily recognize social club members. They speak and act more reserved than some other personality types, especially when they first meet you. Their automobiles are often safety focused; their attire is usually understated and conforming. Women are often the "Plain Jane."

Social club members tend to communicate kinesthetically. They must feel good about you for the two of you to have a successful relationship. You can also appeal to social club members by using testimonials from people who are like them. Focus your presentation on quality, acceptance, and reputation. Ease them forward carefully to counter their resistance to change. Be calm and nonthreatening. Focus on their feelings and relationships.

Focus your presentation on quality, acceptance, and reputation. Be calm and nonthreatening.

Take frequent breaks from business because buying a home is likely to be a stressful situation for social club members. The breaks will help them relax. Reassure them that buying the home is a positive step, and provide support and understanding to help them overcome their fears. They are depending on you to make them feel that everything will be all right.

Social club members are great listeners, reflecting their concern for others. However, they will need time to become comfortable with you before they will act. Because they often lack confidence in their decision-making ability, others probably will be involved in a transaction.

For me, the social club member is the most challenging profile to work with. There is not an ounce of social club member in me. Once when I was the prospective buyer (I was relocating to the east central Florida division of Centex Homes and was searching for a home), I was referred to a Realtor who somehow didn't recognize me as an authority figure. Instead, she treated me like a social club member. As we were visiting communities during the driving frenzy stage, she told me, "You'll just love this neighborhood. It's a little street with only a few homes that ends in a cul-de-sac. At Christmastime, all the mothers assign crafts and determine how all of the homes will be decorated. Then the husbands just seem to do what their wives decide. There are more people who visit this street to see the Christmas decorations all coordinated among the homes. They refer to this street as Candy Cane Lane."

Well, *oh my;* it was as if you just told me that I would be moving to Stepford. I am not a Candy Cane Laner. Conforming to everybody? Hanging out with all the moms? Coordinating Christmas decorations? You have got to be kidding me. That is the last place a female authority figure would want to live. Needless to say, I found another Realtor.

Bean Counter

Bean counter personalities are logical, organized, meticulous, and perfectionist. Like social club members, bean counters avoid risk. They need all of the details before they will decide to buy a home. Unfortunately, they can get so wrapped up in the details that they forget the big picture. You can recognize bean counters because they focus entirely on their own agenda. They are neither responsive to your needs nor assertive in their approach to others. Their automobiles are likely to be no-nonsense as well, such as Toyotas, Hondas, or other brands known for reliability and good gas mileage. Bean counters are typically highly educated and intelligent and their attire may reflect that.

As a sales associate, you are only as valuable to a bean counter as the timeliness and accuracy of the information that you provide to them. Therefore, you appeal to a bean counter by being thorough and knowledgeable. Your presentation to a bean counter should be methodical and factual. The more copious details you can provide, the better. Testimonials, test results, and other data will help you persuade the bean counter. Bean counters will find printed materials such as drawings, plans, and specifications helpful in their decision making. Give them copies of the home plan with the correct garage orientation before taking them on a model tour.

Because they pride themselves on making wise decisions, bean counters' biggest fear is making the wrong decision. Help them draw the correct, logical conclusion. Allow time for them to think about and analyze the information you provide. Bean counters think before they speak, so allow for silence between sentences. Bean counters are seldom visual learners and tend to more often be auditory or kinesthetic learners. For both learning styles, put everything in writing. All prospects filter information that they hear and tend to recall only what was important to them when they heard the information. But for auditory prospects, written words are a very effective means to reiterate what you have presented or to provide additional information that you were unable to present. For kinesthetic learners, having proof of what was said helps them to feel comfortable with what they heard.

Although this is not my strongest style, it is not my weakest, which allows me to work with this style quite effectively. However, the over-the-top bean counter is still a challenge. For example, when I was a sales associate for a community in Temple Terrace, Florida, I worked with a bean counter couple that was considering purchasing a two-story home in which the family room was open to the second-story loft. The details I had to provide, including the pitch of the vaulted ceiling, and the number of other questions I had to answer seemed incomprehensible. With each question they asked, I would reply, "Why is this important?" This question frustrated them. I didn't understand the level of detail they required to move forward. I found it difficult to justify why I needed to provide it. Ultimately, they did purchase the home, but I still remember them as the customers that were not worth the sales commission.

If you are in sales, then you probably are not a bean counter and working with this personality type will be a struggle. But remember, you don't need to understand why bean counters need information in order to provide it—with accuracy, in detail, and in writing. If you follow this basic rule, you will be able to work effectively with your share of bean counters.

Sensory Dominance

Just as there are four main personality types, there are many different learning styles characterized by distinct sensory dominance. Sensory dominance includes sight, sound, and touch. For example, a person whose dominant sense is sight understands more readily if they can see something. Education parlance refers to this person as being a "visual learner." Other people may be "auditory learners"—they gravitate to the spoken word and tend to perform well in traditional educational settings. Still others are "kinesthetic." These people are generally good athletes because they have a well-developed sense of how their bodies and objects move within a space. You can expect to encounter each learning style among buyers. In general, about 50% of your prospects will be visual learners, and the remaining half will be divided equally between auditory and kinesthetic learners.

Visual people notice everything that relates to image: a brochure, company signage, community entrance, and finally, the community and homes themselves. Because visual people may comprise as much as half of a builder's clientele, it's obvious why cleanliness, beauty, and attention to detail are important factors to consider in showing your communities in the best possible light to the greatest number of people.

You can sometimes discern a prospect's dominant sense by listening to their language. Then, you can gear your presentation style and word choices to that sense. For example, if a prospect says they can't picture how their furniture would look in a home, you should respond to them using words that reference seeing, such as, "Let me see if I can help you visualize that."

Prospects who are kinesthetic learners would probably express the same concern differently. They might say, "I don't know how my furniture would feel in this room." If you respond to this prospect in the same way as with a visual learner, you risk disconnecting from them. Instead, you might say, "Maybe I can help you understand the atmosphere your furniture would create."

Other useful guidelines for customizing your sales presentations and demonstrations to your prospects' learning and communication needs are as follows:

Visual Learners

With their well-developed sense of sight, visual people think and remember through pictures and learn best from visual displays. Seeing a completed model or inventory home may be an essential prelude to a purchase. Interestingly, visual people are also often highly energetic and they like to look good. As a sales associate, dressing professionally is always important to making a good first impression, but it is especially important with visual prospects. To them, image is everything.

Anything you can communicate to a visual prospect using a picture rather than words should be part of your presentation. For example, if you are trying to help your visual prospect picture a to-be-built home without having the benefit of a model, show them photos of a prior model or inventory home rather than just providing room dimensions, a verbal description, and a home plan or blueprint. If you are trying to help your visual prospect understand distance to schools, work, shopping, or other locations, show them on a map instead of merely providing verbal directions.

When you must rely on words only, strive to paint mental pictures using colorful adjectives and active verbs. Your influence with visual learners will be proportionate to the vividness of the picture you create for them.

One other interesting thing to note about visual learners is how they use their eyes not just to see but as tools to imagine. If your visual prospects look up and to the right, they are using their creative side and trying to imagine how something might look. If you recognize this, you can assist them better by providing them additional information or other pictures that will help them create this visual image.

When they look up and to the left, they are usually tapping into their memory, trying to recall something important and relevant to a current situation. Knowing this may help you recognize if a prospect is telling the truth. For example, imagine that you have asked them whether they have visited with a loan officer to examine the monthly and initial investment associated with a home in a given price range. If they look up and to the left, they are likely recalling what they learned from the lender. If they look up and to the right, they may be creating a story to tell you.

Table 4.1 lists words and phrases that will appeal to visual learners.

You can also help visually dominant customers by writing things down for them. Although written words are not their primary means of learning new information, the words can cue them to recall what they saw after they have left your model center.

TABLE 4.1 What to Say to a Visual Learner

Visualize . . .	Observe . . .
Imagine how this will . . .	Look at . . .
How does this look?	See . . .
Let's take a look.	Let me show you . . .
Is that clear to you?	Picture . . .
Can you see what I mean?	

Auditory Learners

Auditory learners, those whose dominant sense is hearing, learn by interpreting tone of voice, pitch, rapidity or slowness of speech, and other nuances. Therefore, you must tell an auditory person important facts rather than just giving them information in writing. The good news for salespeople who don't have a model home to show is that auditory people love to hear about your offering, but they don't necessarily need to see it. However, a company's reputation will truly precede it with this group of prospects as they listen closely and place a high value on what others say about your community and company.

Auditory-dominant people may "think out loud" because they find it easier to organize their thoughts when they hear them. They are good conversationalists but may speak slower than visual people. They also are usually sensitive to voice inflection. Understand that they may have difficulty making eye contact; they are concentrating on your words and inflection rather than body language. Don't pressure them to make eye contact with you. Don't speak too quickly. Give them time to process what they hear.

When auditory-dominant people imagine, they look horizontally to the right. When they are remembering, they look to the left. When they think about what they are going to communicate, the words that they are going to use, and how they are going to say something, they look down and to the left.

If you are asking a prospect a fact-seeking question, you would expect them to tap into their memory and their eyes would shift to the left. However, if they look to the right, they are using their imagination instead, which means you're going to get a story rather than the facts.

Table 4.2 lists some words and phrases that would be pleasing to auditory learners.

TABLE 4.2 What to Say to an Auditory Learner

Listen . . .	Comprehend . . .
Hear . . .	Have a handle on . . .
I understand . . .	Doesn't that sound good?
It sounds to me . . .	Shall I talk to you about . . . ?

To ensure that you deliver a winning presentation or demonstration to an auditory person, vary your tone, volume, pitch, and rate of speech to accentuate important points. Auditory prospects will pay as much attention, if not more, to how you speak as to what you say.

In addition, share testimonials and stories orally with auditory people. If you allow auditory people to hear the words rather than having to read them, you will have a better chance of attracting and maintaining their attention. Providing them with an audio CD is a better means of communicating with them than giving them materials they would have to read.

After they leave your community, follow up with these prospects by telephone rather than e-mail unless you are responding to an e-mail message from them. Ultimately, they want to hear a voice. When you do follow up with them, remember that the auditory person hears and remembers everything as if he or she were replaying a recording. Therefore, provide them with stimulating and inspiring words that they can replay long after their visit.

Kinesthetic Learners

Kinesthetic-dominant people learn most readily through hands-on experience. Sensations and emotions are very important in their world. They gain insight by feeling things both physically and emotionally. Therefore, you must first make them physically comfortable and then tap into their emotions to persuade them to buy.

Kinesthetic-dominant people often speak slowly. They communicate best with others when they are nearby. Therefore, they prefer face-to-face communication instead of telephone or e-mail. However, they are not comfortable with constant eye contact, so glance downward occasionally when speaking to them. The kinesthetic-dominant prospect looks down in order to tap into their emotions. If you do so as well, they will know that you are emotionally involved in your product.

Kinesthetic-dominant people need to explore actively. Encourage them to use an appliance, feel the wood cabinets, touch the granite countertop.

At the same time, kinesthetic-dominant people need to explore actively. They have difficulty sitting still for long periods. Therefore, engage them in your presentations and demonstrations. Give them a brochure that they can write on. As you might have guessed, kinesthetic-dominant people love to touch products and feel textures, so invite them to do so in your model homes. Encourage them to use an appliance, feel the wood cabinets, touch the granite countertop, walk around the yard, and sit on the couch.

Kinesthetic-dominant people like to touch and be touched. They will take your hand, touch your arm, and pat you on the shoulder. They will shake hands with you using both of their hands for what may seem like eternity to a person who is not kinesthetic dominant. After you take a deposit to reserve a home or finalize a contract with a kinesthetic dominant person, be sure to shake hands. Although it is important to avoid hurting anyone's feelings, it is especially important with a kinesthetic-dominant person because they are more sensitive and make decisions using emotion more than visual and auditory learners do.

Table 4.3 provides a list of words and phrases that are attractive to kinesthetic learners.

TABLE 4.3 What to Say to a Kinesthetic Learner

I feel good about . . .	My gut tells me . . .
It seems OK to me . . .	Are you comfortable?
I sense something . . .	How do you feel about . . . ?

Treating kinesthetic-dominant people as friends will help you build rapport with them. Have you heard the expression, "People don't care what you know until they know that you care"? That observation is particularly apt with the kinesthetic-dominant person. Moreover, kinesthetic-dominant people like to feel as if they're among friends in their communities. Therefore, tell them moving, emotional testimonials about the impact that owning a home in your community has had on people like them.

Follow Their Lead

I'm a strong visual learner and somewhat of an auditory learner, as well. I am not a kinesthetic learner, and candidly, early in my career I struggled significantly to connect with people who are. I had next to no patience with people for whom everything had to "feel right." Fortunately, however, I'm also results oriented. I quickly understood that although there was a specific personality type I didn't click very well with, I could either choose to accept my weakness in this area—and risk losing sales—or change my behavior when I recognized this type of personality. One technique that worked for me was to pretend that the prospect was my sibling or parent and I was consulting with them on the possible transaction. I became more patient and was able to pay more attention to the prospect's feelings.

You must similarly practice communicating in a variety of ways in order to connect with prospects by tapping into their particular learning style. This technique is how good teachers inspire their students, and it is one way to inspire your prospects. To build rapport and maintain interest in your product, you must enter your prospect's world. Your job is to understand prospects even better than they understand themselves, and then use their preferred communication methods to connect with them. When your prospect knows you understand them, they will trust you more and, therefore, be more likely to buy a home from you.

Each of us is as unique as a snowflake, different from each other and different from you. So don't count on prospects adjusting who they are in order to communicate better with you. A professional sales associate accepts people for who they are and adjusts like a chameleon to be compatible with their prospect. If you can master this skill, you will not only achieve greater success in sales, you will also improve each customer's experience and your personal job satisfaction.

If your prospect is outgoing, approach them more assertively. If your prospect is reserved, take a more reserved approach. Treating everyone with respect and quality service is essential, but adjusting your style to be compatible with your prospects and customers will greatly increase your chances of being successful with them.

5

Body Language
and Word Choice

*W*e communicate with others through our words, our body language, and our tone of voice. Therefore, in addition to becoming comfortable with various personality types and adept at appealing to a prospect's dominant sense or learning style, top sales associates use appropriate vocabulary and effective body language. Communicating effectively entails practice.

Read the following sentence and then punctuate it with two commas.

Woman without her man is nothing.

How did you punctuate the sentence? Depending on your perspective, you could have done it one of two ways. As you will see, each one gives the sentence a distinct meaning that is the opposite of the other:

Woman, without her, man is nothing.

Woman, without her man, is nothing.

In this written example, the punctuation impacts meaning significantly.

In oral communication, we use other tools to convey the proper message. Amazingly, only 7% of our meaning is conveyed by the words we use. The remaining 93% of our meaning is conveyed through body language and tone of voice. In other words, *how* we say something can be more important than the words we use.

Albert Mehrabian, professor emeritus of psychology at UCLA, earned fame for his studies of verbal and nonverbal communication. He found that face-to-face communication uses three elements to convey meaning and these elements are of the following relative importance[5]:

- 7% of the meaning conveyed depends on the words used.
- 38% of the meaning conveyed depends on tone of voice.
- 55% of the meaning conveyed depends on our body language.

We are communicating all of the time with everyone we encounter, even if we are not speaking.

In the 1970s, Richard Bandler and John Grinder created the Neurolinguistic Programming (NLP)[6] communication model based on the study of language, communication, and personal change. They based their model on the practices of three successful psychotherapists: Fritz Perls (Gestalt psychology), Virginia Satir (family systems therapy), and Milton H. Erickson (clinical hypnosis). Bandler's and Grinder's goal was to determine and model the successful behavior and communication patterns of these three individuals.

NLP improves your ability to connect instantly with another person by developing rapport and modeling how they react to specific situations. People tend to feel more comfortable with others like themselves. This comfort allows a prosperous business relationship to develop because the other party believes that your best interests are consistent with theirs. In addition, NLP has shown that your eyes are strong clues to what you are thinking and, instinctively, prospects recognize this attribute.

Because we all communicate primarily through our body language, our posture must be confident, our breathing must be relaxed, and our eye movements must be steady. Because these behaviors model comfort and confidence, they will help your prospects feel comfortable and confident.

Matching and Mirroring

One way to build rapport with prospects, or with anyone for that matter, is to match and mirror their body language, vocabulary, and tone of voice. You discreetly do the same thing with your body as they are doing with theirs. If they were to place their hand on their hip while talking with you, you might casually and naturally place your hand on your hip. "Matching" would be placing your right hand on your right hip if he does the same. "Mirroring" would be placing your left hand on your left hip if his right hand is on his right hip, as if you are creating a mirror image. If handled correctly, creating a physically similar position with the person you are speaking with can create a subconscious connection between you.

> If handled correctly, creating a physically similar position with the person you are speaking with can create a subconscious connection between you.

Practice this technique with caution, however, so you don't offend someone by appearing to imitate them to be humorous. There are appropriate and inappropriate times and places to apply matching and mirroring techniques. Matching another's sense of urgency when there is conflict tends to always be beneficial to the relationship but matching or mirroring body language in these circumstances is not.

You can see examples of how matching and mirroring behavior occurs naturally and instinctively among people who already know each other. The next time you are in a public place, just observe. Watch how people who are connected match and mirror instinctively. Even if they are in a larger group, you can usually see which ones are couples. They send out signals not just by touching each other but through their postures and hand movements. Body language is our instinctive way of telling someone we're either connecting with them or we're not. If people talk with their hands, watch their hand movements closely and use similar movements. For example, if someone uses an open-handed gesture while talking, don't use a closed-hand gesture.

Make sure to be specific. Remember that your physical presence represents more than half of your message and your leg, arm, and head positions are a significant part of your overall body language.

If your prospect sits back and crosses her legs, do the same. If your prospect enters your sales office at a brisk pace with his arms comfortably at his sides and his legs comfortably shoulder width apart, you should approach them decisively to show that you're open as well. Do this by standing with your legs shoulder width apart and toes pointing slightly outward with your arms and hands open rather than folded, clenched, or in your pockets. Lean forward when shaking hands.

Some people are masters, either consciously or unconsciously, of matching and mirroring others. These people are often social and well liked. However, if they are using their skill to manipulate people, their popularity won't last long. This is a powerful tool when used with integrity, but it can backfire if it is used in negative ways. If you use this communication skill to convey information to others that will ultimately benefit them, then you will improve your ability to build rapport and your sales. However, if your intent is manipulative or malicious, you will, instead, destroy relationships.

Matching and mirroring also works effectively with vocal intonation and vocabulary. For example, if your prospect speaks quickly but in a monotone, you might want to speed up your presentation and modulate your inflection. If your prospect refers to a sliding glass door as a door wall and to a study as a den or library, you can do the same. Remember, when it comes to building rapport, people like people who are like themselves.

Empowering Terminology

Just as your thoughts shape your outlook, your words can change the mood of a prospect in an instant. Words help us create pictures in the mind of another person, and when we choose our words carefully, they can help prospects move forward with a purchase decision. The wrong words, however, can unravel a potential sale. When customers feel confident about us and our homes, they are likely to want to move forward with a purchase. On the other hand, your words can erode their confidence and instill fear in them. When that happens, they will pull away.

As you shape your beliefs to be success oriented and you begin to think in more positive terms, you can also improve your sales performance by practicing using words and phrases that will empower your prospects to move toward a purchase.

For example, compare these two statements:

- ◆ "I assist families in finding just the right new home in the Summerwood neighborhood."
- ◆ "I sell houses to prospects in the Summerwood subdivision."

The first statement conveys the sense of ownership that families living in Summerwood feel as a result of their home purchases. The prospect pictures a community with happy families living in their perfect homes. In contrast, the second sentence uses sales jargon and focuses on making a commission rather than on meeting a customer's needs. A single sentence can either convey warm and fuzzy feelings of owning the American dream or trigger customer anxiety about making a purchase. Therefore, choose your words carefully in order to encourage your customers to want your home and community.

Here are some additional examples of words and phrases that you can substitute in order to empower the customer to buy.

Buy vs. Own

People don't want to buy, they want to own. Think about it. To buy means they have to give up their hard-earned money whereas ownership is a privilege and an investment the owners will recoup with increased wealth in the long run. Which of the following questions do you respond to more positively?

- "Would you like to *buy* a home?"
- "Would you like to *own* a home?"

Families vs. People or Prospects

As a sales consultant, you serve families. A family unit can be one person or it may include many people. In either case, the word family is much friendlier and more empowering than the word "people" or the forbidden term, "prospects." "Family" is a word that brings back happy memories whereas "prospect" is a word that reminds the customer that he represents your next commission check. Instead of saying, "I worked with a prospect from Michigan the other day," you should say, "I worked with a family from Michigan the other day."

House vs. Home

"A house is not a home," as the song goes. A house is an object whereas a home is a living, breathing environment. Don't use the word "house" when talking about your homes because it lacks the warmth of a home. Say, "We have a home available on this site," instead of saying, "We have a house available on this lot."

Subdivision vs. Community or Neighborhood

You build in "neighborhoods" or "communities," not "subdivisions." The word subdivision conjures up visions of greedy developers making a profit from prospects. A neighborhood, on the other hand, is a community where families gather and develop connections and friendships. Look at the following two statements:

- ◆ "The subdivision includes a variety of lots."
- ◆ "Our neighborhood includes a variety of home sites."

Which one would resonate with you as a customer?

Standard vs. Included Feature

With seemingly limitless possibilities and endless options today, nobody wants a standard anything. Standard describes an average product and something that most people already have rather than something desirable because it is special. An included feature, however, is one that adds value to a product. When a customer receives an included feature, he is getting something of value for free. Who doesn't like to receive a gift? Instead of telling a customer that "ceramic tile flooring is a standard feature," tell them, "the ceramic tile flooring is an included feature" of your homes.

Spec vs. Available Home

A spec is something that builders build because they are speculating. Speculating isn't a very wise thing to do, and it usually means discounting. Inventory, on the other hand, is a wise investment for most businesses as it is carefully planned construction that responds to consumer demand. If you tell a customer that you have a spec home for sale, he will assume that you are motivated to discount the property. Therefore, instead of telling him that you have a spec house to sell, say, "We have an available home on this site."

Payment vs. Investment, Funds, or Amount

As discussed previously, a home is a sound investment with a reliable return whereas a payment is required to retire debt. Debt is a financial burden that most people do not want. On the other hand, most people enjoy making wise investments. Therefore, substitute the words "monthly investment" or "monthly amount" for "monthly payment" when discussing the financial aspects of homeownership with your customers. When talking to customers about deposits or down payments, discuss these as the initial investment, funds, or amount needed. Instead of saying, "Let's take a look at what you'll need for a down payment," say, "Let's take a look at the initial funds needed."

Contract vs. Agreement or Paperwork

Contracts can be intimidating. Most people want to have an attorney review them. However, we can all feel comfortable making agreements with others without getting a third party involved. Therefore, say "agreement" or "paperwork" instead of contract. Saying "I'll get started on the paperwork" is less intimidating to a customer than saying "I'll get started on the contract."

Lot vs. Home Site, Site, or Parcel

You might have guessed this one already. A "lot" is something a developer develops in subdivisions and the vision that many prospects have is a grid pattern of many lots in a tract-built environment. A "home site" personalizes the site as a unique location for a customer's home. The vision that many prospects have of home sites is larger parcels of unique shapes and sizes. Comparatively large land parcels are typically advertised as sites rather than lots. Therefore, instead of telling customers, "Let's take a look at which lots are available," tell them, "Let's take a look at which home sites are available."

Plat Map vs. Neighborhood Layout or Community Design

A "plat map," or recorded plat, is a government requirement for development. As with industry jargon, although it's OK to use technical terms when talking to planning and zoning officials, it is not appropriate language to use when you are trying to build rapport with customers. Instead, if you talk about "neighborhood layout" and "community design" with families, it helps them appreciate the features and makes them want to live there.

They can picture how families will interact with one another and they begin to see themselves in their new homes. Therefore, don't show them a "plat map"; show them your "neighborhood layout."

Deal vs. Opportunity

Have you really ever gotten a great deal? The word "deal" has the ring of a bad commercial by a used car salesman. In fact, you may as well substitute the word "scam" in a customer's mind. However, nobody wants to pass up an opportunity to make a great investment that will pay off in the long run. A limited offering conveys exclusivity and a well-timed purchase. Instead of asking a customer to "Let me tell you about a great deal," say, "Let me tell you about a great opportunity."

Pitch vs. Presentation, Demonstration, or Show

The word "pitch" is an outdated and inappropriate term for a sales presentation. It conveys slick advertising designed to trick a prospect into buying something they may not want or need. On the other hand, a "presentation" or "demonstration" is an informational tool designed to benefit the customer. I actually prefer to just use the word "show" when asking a buyer's permission to present or demonstrate homes, communities, and features. In interacting with potential buyers, I will simply say, "I'd like to show you the special features in this home."

Elevation vs. Exterior Design

To most people, the term "elevation" means the height of an object above a plane. Many people will not understand this industry term that indicates the exterior design of a home. Therefore, do not use this jargon with prospects. Instead of saying, "We have three elevations for each of our home plans," say, "We have three exterior designs for each of our home plans."

Selling vs. Assisting

Finally, professional salespeople understand that people don't want to be sold on anything; instead, they want assistance in making informed decisions. The following are examples of what to say and what not to say when discussing your work with customers. Don't say, "I sold the Pinehurst plan to the Rodgers just two doors down." Tell your customer, "I assisted the Rodgers family just two doors down with their decision to own a Pinehurst."

Paint Positive Pictures

The words you choose create pictures in prospects' minds and these pictures either will bring them closer to the closing table or drive them away. When developing your presentations, think about the images your words create and avoid using words that conjure up negative images for prospects. When used properly, your language will not only improve your professionalism, it will empower your prospects to move forward.

6

Valuable Qualifying Questions and Techniques

You have two ears and one mouth, and in sales, these should be used proportionally. To succeed in sales, you must listen to and engage prospects in your presentations. To be successful sharing features and benefits with prospects, demonstrating your homes, and showcasing home sites, you must understand what your customers already have, as well as what they like and don't like about what they have. If you don't understand the customer, you might share the benefits of a particular feature, such as a pest defense system, only to learn that the prospect already has the same system in their existing home. You would introduce the pest defense system differently if you knew something about the buyer's current home; don't you agree?

To maintain prospects' interest in your presentations and add value to the time they spend with you, share something new and exciting with them rather than what they already know. To discover what they know and don't know about the benefits of your home features, deliver your presentation conversationally, interspersing questions to help you assess what your buyer is looking for. This inquisitive technique will provide insight into what they already have. Your questions should be worded objectively so that they elicit a genuine response. Asking leading questions that bring your prospects to a conclusion you desire instead of what they want is an archaic sales technique designed to manipulate prospects, rather than help them solve a problem or fulfill a need.

As discussed in chapter 2 in the section "Second Round Eliminations," avoid asking, "Is this your first visit to . . . ?" early in the buying process as it is merely a self-serving "sales" question. Prospects have learned that if they are visiting for the first time, the sales associate will cling to them. On the other hand, prospects have learned that if they say they have worked with someone else, they will be left alone to tour the models without a sales associate. In other words, asking about prior visits does nothing to help you build rapport with a prospect. Instead, by prompting a prospect to talk about their preferences, you engage them in the home buying experience and have more control over the conversation. By involving your prospects in the presentation, they are more attentive and you are able to learn what they value so that you can adapt your presentation to their needs.

Let's look at how to apply valuable qualifying questions and techniques to educate a buyer about a real home feature—a radiant barrier included in every home your builder sells. To convey the value of this feature, you need to know if prospects currently have a radiant barrier in their home and what other types of energy-efficient features they may be familiar with. Knowing how long they've lived in their current home may tell you whether they have this feature and others. Ask the following questions:

- How long have you lived in your current home?
- Have you been introduced to the latest energy-saving products that are available for new homes?
- Do you know what the R-value rating is for the insulation you have in your current home?

These questions will engage prospects in your presentation and encourage them to talk to you. Then you can adjust your presentation to ensure that you are telling them something new and exciting.

Qualifying questions can address the area in which your homes are located, the neighborhood layout, home site, home, financing, builder, and general areas that impact a home purchase. You can adapt questions from the following list for your presentations to help you understand your prospect's needs and desires.

Questions about the Area

- How long have you lived in the area?
- Do you work outside of the home?
- How far would you be driving from [your community name] to work?
- Do you need to know the route from our community to places you regularly go?
- How far is your current home from [your community name]?

Neighborhood Layout Questions

- Have you considered whether you would prefer to have the privacy of a conservation or pond site, or do you prefer to have the security of neighbors all around you with an interior site?
- Do you have any special requirement for your community?
- Have you considered which direction you'd like your home to face?
- Have you had an opportunity to drive through our community?
- Was there something you saw that you'd like to learn more about?

Home Site Questions

- Are you considering installing a pool?
- Can you tell me a little bit about the home site you currently have?
- How important is privacy in your choice of home sites?
- Are you concerned mainly with privacy or with the size of the yard?

Questions about Current and Future Home

- How many bedrooms do you currently have?
- Do you currently have a formal living room as well as a family room or a great room?
- Do you have a preference as to where you'd like to have the sun rise and set in relation to your family room?

- Have you seen a home so far that you really liked?
  If they answer yes to the previous question, ask:
- What prevented you from moving forward with it?
- This home has four bedrooms; how many bedrooms would actually suit your needs?
- Can you share with me a little about your current home and what you like and don't like about it?
- Do you have any special requirements for your new home?
- Do you prefer formal areas in addition to having a family room, or do you prefer to have one living area?
- What type of bedroom and bath configuration are you looking for?
- Why don't we take a look at our neighborhood layout to see which sites can accommodate this home?
- Whose bedroom would this be?
- How would your furniture feel in this room?
- If you decide on the [model], which options do you think you'd like?

Builder-Focused Questions

- Does the builder's reputation play a part in your choice of builders?
- Are you familiar with [builder]?

Financing Questions

- What price range are you considering?
- We are priced from [X] to [Z]. Is that about what you were looking for in a home price?
- Have you had an opportunity to look at the monthly and initial funds required for a home in this price range?
- Have you applied for a home loan before?

General Qualifying Questions

- How soon are you planning to move after you find the right home?
- What prompted you to consider a new home?

- Is there anyone other than yourself who needs to be involved in this process?
- Have you had an opportunity to visit our Web site?
- Are you familiar with our homes or community?

As you develop your model home demonstration, you will find that qualifying questions will improve its effectiveness. The only way you can become one of the best in the business is to understand your prospects' needs. Artfully asking questions will help get you there. Effective questions will help you learn what your prospects need and want. With this knowledge, you can improve your chances of finding them the right home.

The Greeting, Gallery Presentation, and Demonstration

*A*s you demonstrate your homes, sites, and community, prospects will discover the benefits of your offering. As they become more educated about those benefits, they develop their list of "must-haves." That list will include the benefits that come with owning your home. If that isn't reason enough to demonstrate, consider that demonstrating is part of the rapport-building process that is necessary to gain agreement on a home purchase.

True, there are obstacles to demonstrating. When prospects walk in the sales office, their goal is to get a complete brochure, ditch the sales associate, and tour the models. However, if you add value to their time, you increase the likelihood that they will allow you to be part of their home buying process. When prospects understand that you are there to benefit them, they will open up and provide you with the information you need to find a home that suits them. There are really only six issues the buyer has to make decisions on: location, community, home site, home, builder, and financing. By taking control of your model center and prospects immediately on their first visit, you set the stage to guide them through the entire process.

Prospects sometimes want to tour the models without the sales associate because they believe the sales associate's agenda is self-serving and different from their own. Therefore, prospects believe that touring the models on their own will be more effective and efficient. As a professional sales associate, you must dispel this belief as quickly as possible by allowing visitors to accomplish their agenda, even as you add value to their time. Again, align your selling process with their buying process.

> "There are only four ways to create value: information, entertainment, convenience, and savings."
>
> —JAY WALKER
> *Founder, Priceline.com*

In conveying the financial benefit of owning your home, you must both inform and entertain prospects, starting in the sales gallery. The gallery must be designed so that you can see the parking area and properly prepare for your visitors' arrival. Standing and waiting for prospects looks too eager, even desperate, which is not the right impression to present. Sitting down, on the other hand, conveys a lack of respect for prospects and a lack of interest in their agenda. Ideally, you should approach prospects and greet them professionally as they enter your office.

You can never alter a first impression, which significantly influences rapport. Your attire must be professional. A good general rule is that your clothing should be a step above what your typical prospect would wear to work. If you are in a first-time home buyer community and you wear a business suit, you may intimidate your prospect. On the other hand, if you wear blue jeans, you'll be perceived as unprofessional and possibly even uneducated.

Although a polo shirt and khakis may be appropriate for a sales associate in an active adult community, this attire would be too casual for a sales associate in a move-up community selling million-dollar homes. Consider what your prospect probably wears during their average workday or in their retirement, and take your dress up a notch from that.

A sensitive topic, but an important one, is the way you smell. Any strong smell is offensive, including body odor, smoke, and even cologne or perfume. Make sure you take appropriate steps to ensure that the way you smell is neither overpowering nor offensive.

As prospects enter your office, extend your hand to them. If there is more than one person, generally you will extend your hand to the person nearest to you and then progress down the line to everyone in the group. Handshakes should be fully engaged, unless that would be uncomfortable to your prospect. The "V" that your index finger and thumb make should connect with the "V" of the hand of your prospect. A firm handshake shows confidence. However, sometimes your visitor may not be prepared for a strong, firm handshake. In this event, allow your prospect to lead you to what is comfortable for them. Forcing a handshake that is firm and fully engaged is not wise in trying to develop rapport because a prospect might feel like you want to dominate them. There is no place for domineering sales behavior in model home demonstrations.

As you shake hands with your prospect, greet the person as follows:

SALES ASSOCIATE: "Welcome to Oak Trace. Thank you for stopping in. My name is Tammy, and you are . . . ?"

PROSPECT: "William."

SALES ASSOCIATE: "William, it is a pleasure."

Immediately use the prospect's name, which will help you overcome one of the most obvious barriers to building rapport: remembering names. The sooner you use the prospect's name, the more likely you will be to remember it.

Now remember, *do not* ask prospects if it is their first visit. Try the following script instead:

SALES ASSOCIATE: "How may I help you today?"

PROSPECT: "We're just here to look at your models and get a brochure."

SALES ASSOCIATE: "Wonderful! I can definitely help you with that. Let me quickly show you an overview of what you're about to see in the model."

OR

"Terrific! I knew we built these models for a reason. Let me quickly show you an overview what you're about to see in the model."

Depending upon your prospect's personality, you can use humor to break the ice. Also, notice the sales associate's choice of words. Because the prospect used visual words ("look at"), so does the sales associate ("show" and "see").

Your prospects typically want to see your model homes, but before showing the model, present your home plans to them. Hopefully, the builder has ensured that the home plans have the same garage orientation as your models. After showing the home plans, demonstrate the neighborhood layout and then the area map, or modify the order of your presentation to best fit the prospects' interests. Listen to them, observe their nonverbal cues, and adjust your presentation accordingly. If your prospects have the time and they do not appear impatient to get into the model homes, demonstrating your home plans, neighborhood layout, and area map prior to the model homes will help you gain insight into what they want and need. Often, if prospects see something they desire, they will spend more time in your gallery. However, do not assume that you will have more time than they have indicated.

To gauge their familiarity with your company, ask prospects if they have visited your Web site. Generally, more than 80% of prospects have visited a builder's Web site before stepping into the sales office. The fact that they took the next step of coming to view a model indicates that they saw something there that piqued their interest. Follow up by asking those who have visited the Web site if there is something they specifically want to look at or accomplish with their visit or tour of your models. This follow-up shows them that you care about their agenda and gives you insight into what they want in a new home.

Keep in mind that this order of demonstration is not the order of importance in the selling process. The prospects' desire is often to see home plans first, yet the location and community are typically much more important to their final decision. However, remember that your first objectives are to build rapport and add value to the prospects' visit. By presenting the home plans first, you address the prospects' agenda, and this is a positive step toward building rapport. Your second objective is to be able to demonstrate your models. The following is an example of a script to help you accomplish these objectives.

Home Plan Demonstration

SALES ASSOCIATE: "We have 7 different home styles with a minimum of 2 exterior designs. They range from 1,505 to 2,102 sq. ft. of living space. Is this about what you had in mind?"

PROSPECT: "Yes, that will work."

SALES ASSOCIATE: "The first furnished model that you'll see is the Turnbury. It's 1,897 square feet, has 3 bedrooms, a study, 2 bathrooms, and a 2-car garage. It's priced at $248,900. The second furnished model is the Tidewater. The Tidewater is 2,102 sq. ft. with 4 bedrooms, 2 baths, and a 3-car garage. The base price is $279,400."

"William, may I ask you a question?"

PROSPECT: "Sure."

SALES ASSOCIATE: "I want to ensure that I address what you want to accomplish today. How much time do you have for this visit?"

PROSPECT: "I have about 20 minutes."

SALES ASSOCIATE: "OK. In addition to viewing the models and getting a brochure, is there anything else regarding the location, community, home sites, builder, or financing that you want to make sure to review today?"

If the presentation becomes bogged down in one area, suggest ways to keep within the prospects' allotted time, as in the following example:

SALES ASSOCIATE: "William, this model seems to be of great interest to you, but we still have another model to tour and I'm concerned about our ability to accomplish both in the 20 minutes you have available. Which would you prefer that we focus on?"

The next step is to tour the models. Simply say: "OK, then let's go take a look at our models. Follow me." In sales training jargon, this statement is an "assumptive close"—it assumes that you are going into the model homes with the prospect. It is not acceptable to meet up with prospects after they enter the model on their own. Make it a priority to exit the gallery with prospects.

Neighborhood Layout

Always orient your customer to the neighborhood layout. Explain where the models and parking are in relation to the community entrance as follows:

SALES ASSOCIATE: "If you step over to our neighborhood layout, I will show you how Oak Trace is designed. You entered the community from Thirty-eighth Avenue here, and we're now in this model, with parking across the street. Our second model is right next door, here."

"Oak Trace has a total of 68 home sites with a minimum lot size of 70 × 120 ft. We offer sites that back up to a conservation area as well as to the water. In addition, we have some interior sites if you prefer the security of having neighbors all around you. Have you thought about which type of site you would prefer?"

PROSPECT: "Yes, we really like the privacy of having a conservation area behind us."

SALES ASSOCIATE: "That's good news because we have a few good sites left to choose from. Now, the green represents the families that already live in Oak Trace. The blue are homes under construction and under contract. Homes in red are under construction and available if you require a quicker move-in date than our typical six-month building time. The sites in yellow are available for the home of your choice. Is a six-month building time acceptable or do you need something sooner?"

PROSPECT: "It doesn't really matter. We could wait that long if we had to."

SALES ASSOCIATE: "Okay. That gives you more options and may make things a little easier."

"One of the most exciting things about Oak Trace is the mature trees within the neighborhood. Did you get an opportunity to drive through the community?"

PROSPECT: "Yes, we did. The trees were something that caught our eye."

SALES ASSOCIATE: "Yes, they are beautiful, aren't they? Was there anything else that you saw that was of interest or that you'd like more information about?"

PROSPECT: "Yes, there are a couple of sites at the end of this cul-de-sac we'd like information about."

Area Map

Always orient your customer to the area map. Explain where the community is in relation to the route they took to get to it, as follows:

SALES ASSOCIATE: "Let me take a minute to show you where Oak Trace is in relation to the rest of the world [or to major roads and areas of interest]. Oak Trace is here [point]. You probably came into the neighborhood from State Road 70 up Thirty-third Avenue or from 301 and Thirty-eighth Street."

PROSPECT: "Yes, we came in from 301."

SALES ASSOCIATE: "As you can see, we have a couple different approaches into the neighborhood, which makes it convenient, depending upon where you need to drive. For example, to get to I-75, you'd just go south on Thirty-third to State Road 70 and head east 3.9 miles. You can get there most of the time within 5 to 10 minutes depending on whether you're in rush hour or not. On the other hand, taking Thirty-eighth to 301 makes it easy to get to downtown Bradenton. It's only 4.1 miles away and should take no longer than 10 minutes. U.S. 41 is here, which allows you to get to downtown Sarasota and to the beaches in about 20 minutes.

"William, where would you be driving from Oak Trace to work?"

PROSPECT: "My office is at I-75 and University, right here."

SALES ASSOCIATE: "So, you would likely take State Road 70 to I-75 and go south to University. I would guess that it will take you about 20 to 25 minutes."

PROSPECT: "Yes, that's probably right."

SALES ASSOCIATE: "Martha, do you work outside of the home?"

PROSPECT: "Yes, my office is also downtown." (If the prospect answers "no," it is wise to praise her difficult job in the home.)

SALES ASSOCIATE: "As you can see, we have noted some important locations, including the local schools. May I ask you how many are in your family?"

PROSPECT: "There are four of us."

SALES ASSOCIATE: "Is anyone in the family going to be attending any of these schools?"

PROSPECT: "Yes. We have a son and daughter. They're both in high school."

SALES ASSOCIATE: "Where do they attend now?"

PROSPECT: "They're currently going to Southeast, so it is nice that they would not have to change schools."

SALES ASSOCIATE: "Yes, it is. Other locations of interest include the airport, which is located here. The beaches are here, and you'd basically head to downtown, and then take State Road 64 west to get there. Is there any other location that you travel to frequently that you'd like to see?"

Don't assume because your prospects live nearby that they understand the benefit of your location. You will be amazed at the number of things you can share with your prospects that will increase the desirability of your location.

Make sure to align your selling process with prospects' buying process by adjusting your presentation to what is most important to the buyers so you can accomplish both your objectives and your prospects'. Adjust your presentation so that it aligns with what is most important to the prospects and what they wish to accomplish versus what you think is most important in being able to close. You will learn to sense whether and when to discuss the attributes of your homes and communities.

Demonstrating the tools in your sales gallery as early as possible without deviating from your prospects' agenda will allow you to build rapport and demonstrate the balance of your offering later in your presentation.

Your Builder Story

Your builder story doesn't usually make or break a sale. However, it adds to a prospect's confidence in your builder's ability to deliver. It gives the prospect logical reasons to feel comfortable that your company will be able to perform. The story includes your company's size, history, how long it has been building homes, markets in which it builds, and unique selling proposition. The following are two examples of builder stories.

- ◆ "Taylor Morrison is one of the largest home builders in the United States with more than 280 neighborhoods from Florida to California. We're an international company, too. We build homes in Canada, the United Kingdom, Spain, and Gibraltar. But most important to our home owners is that we're known for our innovative home designs, amenity-filled communities, and customer satisfaction. We have won numerous awards from J.D. Power and Associates and consistently finish in the top 5 in customer satisfaction surveys, reflecting the company's commitment to our customers. Is having a builder that is focused on your satisfaction something you're looking for in the builder that builds your new home?"

- ◆ "Lee Wetherington Homes is a locally owned and operated company founded in 1974 with a very clear mission. We strive to provide you with the best experience in home building. Our goal is to excel in our industry and to exceed your expectations. We have more than 30 years of home building experience and have built more than 2,500 homes in the most prestigious and sought-after communities in Sarasota and Manatee Counties. We are known for exceptional quality and unsurpassed customer satisfaction, even from the most demanding consumers. Our promise to our customers is to provide you with the utmost convenience and service throughout your home building experience and deliver to you a home that exceeds your expectations without a doubt. Does it sound like we might be the builder for you?"

Handling Interruptions

Although a busy sales office with a lot of foot traffic is a welcome situation in the home building industry, sales associates often don't know how to handle interruptions. If you are working with a prospect in your gallery and the telephone rings, do not excuse yourself to answer the phone. Moreover, if other employees enter your sales office, understand that they are less of a priority to your business than your immediate prospect. The entire company relies on your ability to successfully influence prospects to move forward with a home purchase.

If you are confronted with more than one prospect at a time, you can present the tools within your sales office and even demonstrate your models to them simultaneously. However, you cannot effectively sell to two prospects at once. They won't want to answer qualifying questions while others are listening. Therefore, gracefully acknowledge new customers while assessing each prospect's urgency. Then, as you move into your model home, focus most of your time and attention on the prospect with the greatest sense of urgency and the fewest barriers to moving forward with a purchase.

When other prospects, buyers, and current home owners arrive in your office, acknowledge them and quickly assess their needs. Just as an immediate prospect takes precedence over a ringing phone or another employee, current home owners and buyers take precedence over prospects. This preference doesn't mean that you should spend time visiting instead of taking care of your prospects. Just recognize that current owners and buyers already have committed to your company and community so you must ensure that they are satisfied with their choice. Your post-sale attention to owners and buyers will increase long-term customer satisfaction, and therefore, referrals.

As with all demonstrations, the gallery presentation requires practice. One of my favorite sales trainers and bestselling author of *How to Master the Art of Selling,* Tom Hopkins, says "Practice, drill, rehearse . . . Repetition is the mother of skill."

If you are in a community with more than one sales associate, role-play by taking turns as the sales associate and the prospect. Even without another person to role-play with, you can visualize what a prospect might say and do. You will be surprised at how often real prospects respond as you imagined. Get to know the script for your sales gallery presentation better than you know your morning routine. Know it so well that you internalize it and can demonstrate without thinking. This level of competency will pay huge dividends in your being able to

- build rapport
- quickly assess what your prospects want

- conduct more model home demonstrations
- sell more homes

Model Home Demonstrations

Prospects don't leave your model center and go home to make a purchase decision in a vacuum. They will shop competitors and then compare those homes with your demonstration. For this reason, in order to stand out in the customer's decision-making process, you must not only stay in touch with them, as discussed in chapter 3, you also must master all-important demonstration skills.

If you learn to demonstrate your home offering well, you will place yourself ahead of competitors who fear demonstrations because they have not mastered this skill. Moreover, if you work to improve your demonstration skills, you will begin to enjoy demonstrations more and you will want to demonstrate your offering. Self-improvement is the beginning of a winning cycle in which success breeds more success!

Don't Abandon Prospects

Consider what happens when prospects tour your models without you. Have you noticed how quickly they complete their tour? If you're fortunate, there may have been items in the models that grabbed the prospects' attention, but don't confuse attention with interest. The objective is to capture the prospects' interest, which only occurs when you focus that attention. Unless you can hold the prospects' attention *and* stimulate their interest, the prospects will not buy in your neighborhood.

You must demonstrate your models whether or not prospects arrive with a Realtor. In other words, don't assume that Realtors know how to demonstrate better than you can. In most cases, they do not know how. Also, consider that Realtors have their own agenda, and it could be to sell a home other than yours to prospects. Therefore, it is just as important, if not more so, to demonstrate when prospects are accompanied by Realtors. Just be sure to include the Realtors in the process by asking them some of the essential qualifying questions. For example, most Realtors will know how soon prospects are planning on moving, how many bedrooms and baths they desire, and whether they would prefer a one- or two-story home. Feel free to direct obvious questions of this sort to the Realtor. You will find that the Realtor will volunteer much of the information you need once you get them started.

How confident are you that a prospect who is virtually running through your models, with or without a Realtor, will voluntarily focus on anything long enough to realize the unique benefits of your offering? As a professional sales associate, you are obligated to stimulate prospects' interest and thoroughly demonstrate those benefits. If you don't, you are serving neither the builder nor the potential buyer well. Recall that you want to align yourself with buyers' home search process while adding value to their time. Tell customers you plan to add value to their time by touring the model with them as follows:

> SALES ASSOCIATE: "As we tour the models, I will be identifying three things. The first is our included features. These are the features that come with each home here at Oak Trace. I'm also going to point out the optional features. These are the items we have installed in the model that are available to add to your home if you desire. Finally, I will point out the decorator items. These are items that we have installed in the models just to demonstrate the homes' livability. These items are not available for purchase."

The Art and Order of Demonstration

Typically, you will demonstrate the models prior to the home sites because prospects have no reason to view sites until they see a home they would like to live in. Of course, there are exceptions to every rule, but in general prospects must know that your builder can meet their home requirements before they will invest time looking at sites. This doesn't mean that prospects will compromise their site requirements. In fact, with few exceptions, they will compromise on their requirements for the home before compromising their site requirements.

At any rate, think of your rapport building with prospects in the sales office as your one opportunity to earn the right to show them the model. Make that your primary objective. Next, while demonstrating the model, you are earning the right to show them inventory and/or sites, so that must be your primary objective. Finally, after they have selected a home site, you have earned the right to close. Every demonstration step is essential to the process. Remember, prospects decide upon the location, community, home site, home, builder, and financing. You must demonstrate all of these elements well in order to close. Integrate the following elements into your demonstrations and you will become a master at capturing and holding a prospect's interest:

* an understanding of the prospect's communication and personality preferences
* rapport-building questions
* qualifying and discovery questions
* feature, bridge, benefit, and tie-down statements (chapter 8)
* overcoming resistance (chapter 9)
* closing questions (chapter 10)

Model Home

A model home demonstration includes four steps:

1. Opening statement
2. Presentation
   Features and benefits
   Qualifying questions
   Handing resistance
   Trial closes
3. Transition statement
4. Closing question to transition to the next step

You will repeat steps 1 through 3 for each demonstration area of the model home. Step 4 is the final step before closing.

In crafting your demonstrations, keep in mind that first and last impressions are critical memory points for prospects. Therefore, begin and end with impact and sandwich the weakest home features in the middle of each presentation area. Consider the best place to begin, how to end with impact, and how you will use the home's assets to control the demonstration's flow. Strive not to walk and talk at the same time. You will be able to keep prospects focused on what you're discussing instead of where you are going. Instead, walk to the next presentation area only after making your transition statement. Tables 7.1 and 7.2 list opening statements and transition statements for the areas you are likely to demonstrate.

Above all, do not allow prospects to enter the model through the door that leads from the garage because you risk squandering one of a home's obvious assets: its curb appeal. In fact, the entire front exterior of the home and streetscape is your first presentation opportunity.

If your sales office is in the garage of the model home you are going to demonstrate, before exiting the office you may want to acquaint your prospects with the garage like this:

> "The area we're in now would normally be the garage. The location of these windows and doors here is where the garage door would be and you'd enter the home from the garage

TABLE 7.1 Opening Statements

Area	Statement
Foyer	"Isn't the first impression spectacular?"
Formal areas	"As you can see, this home's formal areas are more traditional and set the tone for the entire home."
Family room	"In this area, we've combined the family room and kitchen in a manner that is really convenient, don't you agree?"
Kitchen	"I really hope you love the way this kitchen is designed as much as I do . . . ."
Secondary bedrooms	"Do you see how private this area is, tucked away from the rest of the home?"
Guest bedroom	"Isn't this just perfect for your guests? It's as if they had their own master suite; don't you agree?
Master suite	"Isn't it wonderful?"
Master bathroom	"This design is perfect for couples who have similar schedules, giving you both the space you need even if you're getting ready for work at the same time."
Lanai	"Can you see how this area can easily be used as extended living space?"
Backyard	"This yard gives you all the privacy you need without a lot of yard work. Do you see what I mean?"

TABLE 7.2 Transition Statements

Area	Statement
Family room	"Let's take a look at the area where your family members spend will spend most of their time."
Laundry room	"I think you'll like the location of the laundry room. Let me show you."
Secondary bedrooms	"This plan is ideal for the privacy of everyone, especially because of where the secondary bedrooms are located. Let's take a look."
Unique room	"Next we're going to see something that you wouldn't normally find in a home this size. Follow me."
Guest bedroom	"One of the bedrooms is ideal for guests. It's almost a second master suite. I want you to see what I mean."
Master bedroom	"As I've said before, I have saved the best for last. Let's go take a look at the master suite."
Master Bathroom	"I hope you find where we're going next to be as special as I do. Follow me."
Back Lanai	"The outdoor living space of this home is spectacular. Let's go take a look."
Backyard	"Since we do a lot of outdoor living here, let's go take a look at your backyard."

through the door over there. However, we're going to go this way, so that you can experience the first impression just like your visitors would. Okay?"

The following are possible opening and transition statements for the front exterior of the home:

SALES ASSOCIATE: "Before we enter the home, I'd like to share with you a few of our exterior features . . . . Why don't we take a look inside?"

Then, enter the model through the front door. As you leave your sales office, you should walk out the door ahead of your visitors. Ideally, the office door opens such that as the prospect closes the door, he or she is facing the home. Self-closing hinges are an even better solution because if the prospect doesn't close the door, you won't have to move behind them in order to do so.

Figure 7.1 shows a sample model home demonstration map. You would leave your sales office and stop at each numbered location as follows:

1. Position yourself outside of the home where the prospect, centered in front of the entryway, can view the full exterior design of the home. The farther away from the home you can comfortably position yourself, the better the view of your home's exterior. In addition, make sure that you can view the streetscape of the adjacent homes.

2. Prior to entering the home, stop and remind the prospect of the name of the plan, the number of bedrooms and baths, and the square footage of the living space.

3. Stand in front of the master bedroom. Many prospects will want to immediately view this area of the home, yet it usually is one of the best features so you probably want to end your demonstration with it.

4. The laundry room is not a focal point. You can easily show it on the way to the secondary bedrooms. Position yourself so prospects enter the secondary bedroom area instead.

5–7. The secondary bedrooms and bath are often not central features of the home. You can view them before demonstrating the family room and kitchen.

8. The family room and kitchen are often a home's focal points. Find a location where you can stand and show both areas comfortably. Because these are large rooms with many features to demonstrate, you will move around the rooms.

9. The den, technical or computer center, and pool bath are an easy transition to the outdoor living area.

10. Depending upon the climate, outdoor living areas are often viewed as additional living square footage so be sure to demonstrate them.

11. The size of the yard may be important. If so, and if the model home site is comparable to the typical home site in the community, you can go outside.

12. Entering the master bedroom from the direction of the lanai actually makes the room look larger because most master suites

FIGURE 7.1 Model Home Demonstration Map

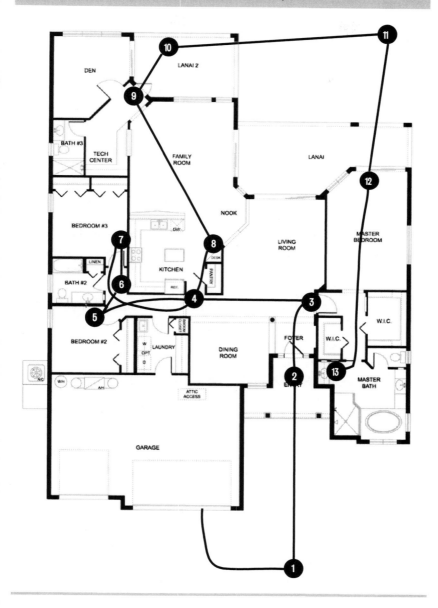

are combined with a spacious bathroom. The ability to see all the way through both areas makes for a dramatic entry into the areas.

13. The master bath is often dramatic and is a wonderful place to end the demonstration.

Throughout your presentation, position yourself to ensure that prospects follow your preplanned route, offer an opening statement for each presentation area, and make a transition statement to lead prospects from one area to the next.

10 Steps to Winning Demonstrations

A proper home demonstration not only helps you to qualify the prospect and improve your rapport, it also allows you to thoroughly understand your prospect. This successful demonstration enhances your relationship, thereby increasing your ability to sell the prospect a home.

The following 10 steps will help you prepare winning demonstrations:

1. Determine the appropriate flow. Remember to start and finish with impact.
2. Map the flow on a home plan including where you are going to stop to demonstrate each area.
3. Walk the models and decide the most logical route.
4. Visualize taking prospects from one area to the next and identify the most appropriate location to stand and demonstrate each room.
5. Determine which features you are going to demonstrate and list them for each room, looking for features that can involve the prospect.
6. Write a feature/bridge/benefit/tie-down statement, as discussed in chapter 8, for every feature you intend to demonstrate.
7. Determine the qualifying questions you are going to ask for each area and write them down.
8. Identify your opening statements for each demonstration area and write them down.

9. Identify your transition statements for each demonstration area and write them down.

10. Plan which trial closes are appropriate in each area you will demonstrate.

Congratulations! You have created the perfect script for an exceptional model home demonstration. Now practice—alone and/or with your business associates and friends—what you have written. Visualize success with every word and gesture. Remember, it is not enough to know what to do, you must do what you know. Practice and apply these techniques and you will experience positive results!

After demonstrating the model home or homes, you may ask a closing question (chapter 10) or suggest taking the next step. The next step will vary based upon the prospect's needs; however, in most cases your goal is to persuade the prospect to view home sites. Doing so will transfer a sense of ownership and make your home unique. In some cases, the prospect will need to review financing. In any case, your objective is to close on whichever is the next step in the prospect's buying process and transition to the transaction that will move the prospect closer to owning one of your homes.

8

Benefits Make the Difference

M any prospects begin their home buying process without really knowing what they want in their new home. Although they may know how many bedrooms they need and how many baths they prefer, they haven't thought through the details of home plan design, home features, or site characteristics. They simply know that their current home is inadequate. The "must-haves" for their new home will unfold as they begin to look at available properties. In addition, most prospects don't know what questions to ask or what features to compare among available homes. Demonstrating your model homes, home sites, community, and location increases the possibility that your offering will have the essentials they are looking for. When prospects know what they want, it is easier for you to find a home that will fulfill their needs. On the other hand, your prospects may never discover the value of your offering if they are left to discover it for themselves.

An essential component of proper demonstrations is ensuring that prospects understand benefits—how their lives will improve if they purchase your home. Allowing prospects to tour models on their own assumes, wrongly, that they will be able to notice all of the included features and be able interpret them as benefits. Therefore, rather than sending buy-ers off on a self-guided tour, a professional sales associate offers them a model home demonstration that explains the benefits of a builder's home features.

Consider the following features displayed in model homes:

- wall and ceiling insulation
- optional or bonus rooms
- pest defense systems
- radon mitigation systems
- radiant barriers
- formed and poured walls
- Thermopane windows

If prospects walk through your model on their own, they will proba-bly overlook all of these important features. If they can't even see the fea-ture, how can they possibly be aware of the benefit the feature provides? Moreover, you not only need to make them aware of the benefit, you need to explain it in terms they will understand and then sell them on it. They need a skilled professional to capture their attention, stimulate their inter-est, and encourage them to move forward with a purchase.

Why do so many sales associates have trouble bringing prospects along in a demonstration? I have found that most sales associates do not know how to hold prospects' attention. Sales associates do not regularly provide prospects with the information they want or need to know. Once you master the skill of developing interest during your demonstrations, you will easily maintain your prospects' attention.

One sure way to arouse prospects' interest is to tell them something new and unusual about a product with which they are already familiar. Keep this in mind as you demonstrate your model homes. They are filled with features that have new and different attributes. Prior to demonstrat-ing your model homes to prospects, walk through the homes yourself with fresh eyes and ask yourself the following questions about everything you see:

- What's different about this?
- How can this change everyday life?
- Is there a way to dramatize this?

◆ How can I involve my prospect actively with this?
◆ Can I show this differently than I have been?
◆ Can my prospect operate this while they're here?
◆ Is there a way I can surprise the prospect with this?
◆ What is the major benefit of this?

Every item in your model home is likely to have at least one benefit and, in some cases, several benefits. Your objective is to demonstrate features that provide the most value to the customers and ensure that your prospects understand these benefits. Figure 8.1 provides a formula to use.

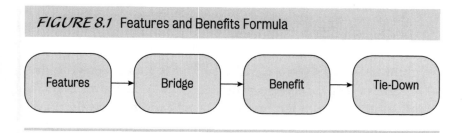

FIGURE 8.1 Features and Benefits Formula

Turning Features into Benefits

Features are the facts that describe a product and how it functions. For example, tile flooring features include its size, color, texture, and specific material such as porcelain. Benefits, on the other hand, describe what the feature will do. For example, you may say, "We offer more than 30 floor tile designs with different colors, textures, and sizes to ensure that your flooring will be able to easily complement your furnishings and décor." Benefits are the "what's in it for me" to prospects. A professional sales associate understands that in order to engage a prospect and ultimately win a sale, you can't just tick off lists of features. Instead, you must follow through by explaining the advantages of the features demonstrated. If the feature adds no living pleasure to the prospect's life, then there is really no point in discussing it.

After listening to your presentations and watching and/or participating in your demonstrations, a prospect should understand how the feature enhances a home's desirability or solves a specific problem. Fortunately, there are bridges that can help you tie a feature to a benefit. These are transitional words and phrases you can learn to use. With practice, you will find that using these bridges is second nature. The following sentences demonstrate how to use bridges (which are italicized in the following examples) to tie features to benefits.

- We include a pest defense system in our home *which allows* you to have your home serviced for pests without the hassle of having to be present for service calls.
- This is a split bedroom plan *which will* provide you and your children with more privacy.
- This is really convenient *because you can* get to work in just minutes.
- Our lender will have a representative here this weekend. *This could possibly* assist you and expedite your approval process if you haven't already found a lender.
- We include a radiant barrier in our homes. *You'll appreciate this because* it will result in lower electric bills because it prevents the Sun's heat from entering your home.
- A safety barrier is included in our pool packages. *This means that* your little ones will always be safe.
- Telephone, network, and cable pre-wires are included in all bedrooms *so that* you're networked from the day you move in.
- We offer 14 different cabinet styles with 2 to 6 colors per style; *therefore, you'll be able to* easily match your décor.
- We've installed slide-out shelves in our kitchen cabinets. *This enables you* easier access to items you have stored in the back of the cabinet.
- I'll be happy to make the appointment for you *so that* if you decide to move forward the process will be expedited.
- We include a security system. *This will assure you* a greater level of safety for your family.
- R-30 insulation is included. *This is important because* ceiling insulation of this thickness ultimately will reduce your electricity costs.
- Most of your personal choices can still be included in this home. *This means that* you can take delivery of your new home in about two months and still personalize it.
- The Nottingham is already permitted on this site. *So if you decide* to move forward, you will reduce the build time on this home by about 45 days.

If you're not sure what the benefit of a specific feature is, ask yourself this question, "If my prospects had this feature, what would it mean to them?" Then use a bridge statement to tie the feature to the benefit.

After you have discussed how your home's various features will benefit the customer, the final step in your demonstration is to gain confirmation, or agreement, that the benefit is worthwhile. You do this by using tie-down questions. An example of a tie-down statement is: "That makes sense, doesn't it?"

Below are many ideas of tie-downs that you can use in your presentations:

- This is a beautiful view; *don't you agree?*
- The trees in this neighborhood are just beautiful; *don't you think?*
- *Wouldn't it* be nice to be able to have the privacy of a split bedroom with teenagers in the home?
- The covered lanai adjacent to such a peaceful background could really be relaxing, *couldn't it?*
- This kitchen that opens to your family area appeals to your desire for entertaining, *doesn't it?*
- This detail really adds to the architectural appeal of the home, *don't you think?*
- This is quite important, *isn't that right?*
- It's important for most of us to have everything convenient to the neighborhood, *isn't it?*
- It seems that we offer many of the selections you were looking for, *wouldn't you agree?*
- *Wasn't it* wonderful when we were growing up to be able to play in the front yards with all of our friends?
- They are beautiful, *aren't they?*
- *Can't you imagine* how wonderful it would be to sit back and admire the sunset with this view?
- The developers really have done a fantastic job of creating the feeling of an established neighborhood, *haven't they?*

See if you can locate the feature, bridge, benefit, and tie-down words in the following sentences:

- "We include a smooth-top range, which allows for easier cleaning. Don't you agree?"

> *feature:* A smooth-top range
> *bridge:* Which allows for
> *benefit:* Easier cleaning
> *tie-down:* Don't you agree?

◆ "R-30 ceiling insulation is installed in all of our homes. This means that you will save money on your electric bill. It is better at insulating your home than standard R-19 and is more environmentally friendly. Isn't that great?"

> *feature:* R-30 ceiling insulation
> *bridge:* This means
> *benefit:* You will save money on your electric bill. It is better at insulating your home than standard R-19 and is more environmentally friendly.
> *tie-down:* Isn't that great?

Some features must be explained before you transition to a benefit statement. The formula for doing this is shown in figure 8.2.

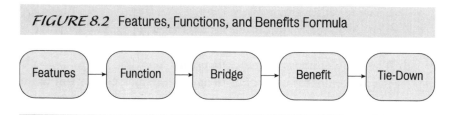

FIGURE 8.2 Features, Functions, and Benefits Formula

You simply add an explanation prior to the bridge that leads to the benefit. A bridge can often precede the function. The following is one example of each scenario.

◆ "Radiant barrier is installed in your ceiling to block the Sun's radiant heat from getting into your attic. This will help keep the temperature cooler and ultimately reduce your electric bill. It's also more environmentally friendly. It feels good when you can do something so simple for the environment; don't you agree?"

> *feature:* Radiant barrier is installed in your ceiling.
> *function:* To block the Sun's radiant heat from getting into your attic
> *bridge:* This will help

> *benefit:* Keep the temperature cooler and ultimately reduce your electric bill. It's also more environmentally friendly
>
> *tie-down:* It feels good when you can do something so simple for the environment; don't you agree?

The following statement reverses the order of the benefit and function:

♦ "We include a pest defense system in your new home, which most people find convenient because you are assured that your home will be serviced without the interruption or inconvenience of having a service representative enter your home. Isn't that a more convenient way to ensure your home stays free of pests?"

> *feature:* We include a pest defense system in your home
>
> *bridge:* Which most people find is
>
> *benefit:* An extreme convenience
>
> *bridge:* Because you can
>
> *function:* Ensure that your home gets serviced without the interruption or inconvenience of having a service representative enter your home
>
> *tie-down:* Isn't that a more convenient way to ensure your home stays free of pests?

Asking a tie-down question about the benefit prior to sharing the feature can increase the impact of your demonstrations because it keeps prospects engaged, which will help them remember your presentation. The following are two examples of using this questioning technique when presenting the pest defense and energy-saving features discussed previously:

♦ "Wouldn't it be convenient if you could ensure that your home stays pest free without the inconvenience of a service representative having to enter your home?"

♦ "Wouldn't it be nice if you could reduce your electrical consumption and therefore your electric bill and help out the environment simultaneously?"

To refine your demonstrations, tour your model homes with worksheet 8.1 and note the features that you and your prospects like most (*see* Appendix).

- Does the room have an exceptional feeling or flow?
- What's special about it?
- How is it different from most of your competitors' homes?
- What is the first reaction that prospects have when they enter the room?

You will see that there are no limitations to the benefits you can discuss. Use your imagination and be creative with your presentations! The following 5-step process will help you develop winning presentations:

1. **Write down** appropriate feature/bridge/benefit/tie-down statements for the unique aspects of every room in each of your models.
2. **Brainstorm** other benefits that don't typically come to mind.
3. **Create** attention-grabbing ways to highlight these benefits without worrying about what prospects' reactions will be. Try everything.
4. **Build** the preceding material into presentations.
5. **Practice** the presentations using role-play and visualization.

I have lain in a bathtub so that my prospects could see how huge it was. I've invited five other people into a shower with me to demonstrate its size. Playful approaches like these interject humor and help break down barriers between you and your prospects. They will pay attention to your presentations and remember you and your homes. You will be amazed at how you will be able to engage your prospects, add value to their time, and persuade them—all of which will lead to more sales.

Overcoming Resistance

esistance typically occurs when prospects are trying to resolve a concern in order to move forward. Therefore, if your prospect is showing resistance, celebrate! They are considering purchasing a home from you.

If your prospect is not interested in your home or community, then they will have no concerns that you can address. However, when a prospect sees an obstacle, voices an objection, or demonstrates resistance to an aspect of the transaction, view it as the feedback you need to help them solve a problem. Your

"Obstacles are those frightful things you see when you take your eyes off the goal."

—HENRY FORD
Inventor

objective is to identify the prospect's core concern and either respond to it or find an alternative solution. Keep in mind that you don't have to react to every concern a prospect voices. Some people just think out loud; this does not necessarily mean that they have a core concern that you must address. Prospects may resist merely to delay making a decision. Knowing when to respond to resistance is an art rather than a science. Watch and listen for both verbal and non-verbal cues a prospect communicates.

Five Steps to Overcoming Resistance

You can apply a 5-step process to overcome resistance, as shown in figure 9.1.

Align

The first step is to align yourself with your prospects. By aligning with them, you take away their defensiveness and work harmoniously with them so they will be open to your perspective. Although alignment can be difficult, it is an essential strategy to cultivate early in the relationship. It will help you later when a prospect's concern is a deal breaker. Following are some ways to align with your prospect:

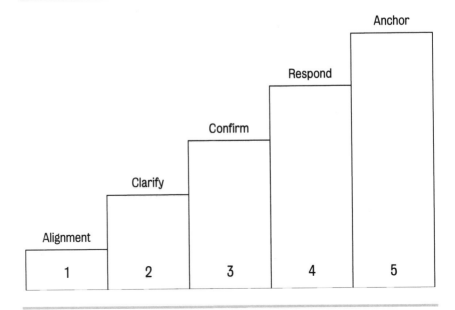

FIGURE 9.1 Handling Resistance

- Agree with the truth if the prospect is stating the truth.
- Agree with the odds if what the customer is saying may be possible.
- Agree in principle if what the customer says makes sense.

If you can't align with the customer on any of these three dimensions, at least demonstrate that you understand his perspective. For example, if your prospect says, "I don't want my children going to Palmetto High School," you can respond, "I completely understand that the schools that service our community play an important role in whether Oak Trace works for you."

You are not agreeing that there is anything wrong with Palmetto High, you are simply agreeing in principle that the prospect must consider schools. Aligning yourself with your prospect moves you away from opposition and toward congruence with the prospect's perspective.

The following are additional examples of statements that can align you with your prospect's objection:

- "Yes, I agree. This premium on this site is higher than most . . . "
- "You may be right."
- "Sure, that makes sense."
- "I can see why you might feel that way."
- "I agree: Location is crucial."
- "That's true. Rates are rising."
- "You are correct. The market has softened compared to 2004 and 2005."

Clarify

After you align with your prospect, the second step in overcoming resistance is to clarify his or her real concern. One of the three following questions can almost always clarify a concern:

- "What is it about _____ that concerns you?"
- "You don't want your children to go to Palmetto High School?" (Repeat the concern back to the prospect with the inflection of a question.)
- "What do you mean?"

Again, using the school example, you could combine the following clarifying questions with the previous alignment statement about Palmetto High School: "I completely understand that the schools that service our community play an important role in whether Oak Trace works for you."

- ◆ "To clarify my understanding, what is it about Palmetto High that concerns you?"
- ◆ "You say you don't want your children going to Palmetto High School. Can you help me understand your position?"
- ◆ "Okay. What do you mean?"

The third response is most effective if used right after the statement of resistance. A lengthy alignment sentence will reduce its impact. Therefore, just answer the prospect's concern with a simple "OK" or no statement at all, and then ask the clarifying question, "What do you mean?"

When asking clarifying questions, you must already have a comfortable relationship with your prospect so they know you are there to help them, not sell them something they don't want. If you have not built significant rapport with the prospect, clarifying questions can sound too pushy or confrontational.

Following your first clarification question, you may want to ask a number of follow-up questions to further clarify the issue and be able to respond adequately to the prospect's concern.

Many sales associates assume the concern and answer an issue that was never an issue to begin with, creating new issues. Again, using the Palmetto High School example, the sales associate may assume that the issue is recent test scores when in reality the prospect is more concerned about travel time to school or that all of his children's friends go to a different high school. In any case, make sure you fully understand a customer's issue before you attempt to respond to it.

As you discuss the customer's concern, mentally classify it into one of the following 9 categories. This classification will help you respond to the concern and understand how to proceed past the confirmation stage.

- ◆ **Major.** This is an uppermost concern and may be one that you cannot comfortably satisfy. For example, the customer's move depends upon a relocation package that he has not yet received.

- **Hidden.** This voiced concern is masking the prospect's genuine concern. For example, a prospect may tell you that the reason he doesn't want his children in Bloomingdale Middle School is the school's test scores, but the real issue is his perception about the demographics.
- **Easy.** A prospect generally presents an easy issue in the form of a simple question that is not very controversial. For example, he may say, "This bedroom seems small. What size is it?"
- **Request for reassurance.** A prospect will often say that there are obstacles to buying when, really, he just wants others' opinions, including yours. For example, he might discuss his commute. You may just need to affirm that the property is within an acceptable distance to work.
- **Request for pressure.** Some prospects are afraid to make a decision so they welcome some pressure; they want someone else to conclude the transaction. A request for pressure is the most desired resistance. It signals that the customer is ready to move forward and you simply need to provide the reason for them to do so. A classic objection which often is a request for pressure is, "We need to think it over." This chapter later addresses in detail how to respond.
- **Request for more information.** A sales associate may be able to resolve this issue simply by providing some documentation. If the concern is that Bloomingdale Middle School doesn't have high enough standardized test scores but you know it does, then providing the correct information can resolve the issue easily.
- **Stall or delay.** Prospects will often stall simply because they want more time to make a decision or because they need to resolve an issue unrelated to the home or community before moving forward. A stall objection is often one that you never have to answer.
- **Doubt.** Many prospective buyers are afraid of making a bad decision or doubt their ability to make a wise decision. People want to avoid pain and attain pleasure. If a prospect is afraid or doubtful, then we have not provided the vision of enough pleasure to outweigh the pain.
- **Prejudice.** Prejudiced resistance is an objection over which you have no influence. You cannot force a potential home buyer to

change deeply held beliefs or judgments, no matter how wrong they are. For example, if a prospect refuses to consider an interior home site because he or she believes interior sites have less resale value, you will not change this perception, even if the home otherwise suits the family.

Confirm

Once you understand the issue and have classified it properly, you can paraphrase your customer's concern to acknowledge that you heard and understand it. For example, the sales associate in the above example could say, "So, your concern about having your children attend Palmetto High is the proximity of the school to the community and your office; is that correct?"

Respond

The response requires the most preparation but also provides the best creative opportunity for countering resistance. Fortunately, you can prepare responses well in advance of when you need them by looking objectively at your community or communities and determining likely areas of concern for most prospects. Most communities will garner four to six major objections that require advance planning. These objections may relate to home sites, homes, community, location, builder, and financing. Some typical concerns that would be considered major objections are as follows:

1. The community has a noise concern such as a highway or airplane traffic.
2. The traffic window to the community is not visually attractive.
3. The school district is not rated strong for the area.
4. The home sites back to something that is not visually pleasing such as power lines or commercial development.
5. The price is too high.
6. The preferred lender is not desirable.
7. The home site is too small.

Preparing to respond to concerns like these is essential to effectively handling resistance. You can craft responses to known concerns, such as the seven above, as well as to unanticipated concerns. Before formulating a response, though, remember to uncover the core concern of an objection. As mentioned previously, effective responses (or whether to respond at all) hinge on the type of resistance. For example, you usually must address major issues, hidden issues, and requests for more information effectively before you can close. The sooner these issues are resolved, the more likely you are to get a closing opportunity. Easy issues, requests for reassurance, and doubt can be addressed at any time. In fact, delaying a response to these issues is sometimes the best approach because they may resolve themselves as the prospect becomes more comfortable with the idea of buying a home. Stalls or delays, likewise, will often evaporate on their own, so you may not need to address them.

Sometimes, a customer will present an unanticipated objection that you will have to respond to spontaneously. Learning this skill requires practice. The more you practice your known objections and spend time crafting responses to new objections, the better you will become in responding spontaneously. Until you are comfortable with doing so, it is often best to defer answering the concern. It is OK to tell your prospect that he has a good point and that you will get back to him.

It is OK to tell your prospect that he has a good point and that you will get back to him.

Finally, don't waste time trying to fight a prospect's prejudice; you will not change his mind. Instead, show him a home or home site that resolves the concern. If the prejudice is one that involves a protected class under equal housing opportunity laws, tell prospects that you and your company fully comply with equal housing opportunity requirements, and then move on.

When you must address an obstacle, you can reframe or dilute the concern, minimize its importance, or convert a negative attribute into a positive one. Consider using third-party testimonials, countering with facts, providing alternatives, or listing the positives and negatives associated with purchasing the home. Here are some examples:

- ♦ "This bedroom is too small" is a common complaint about secondary bedrooms. Simply asking, "What would you use this room for?" can dilute the concern. If the room is going to be a guest room or one for a small child, then this question alone can dilute the concern. If the issue arises again you will need to address it in more detail; otherwise, consider it a minor issue that will evaporate as prospects move closer to making a decision.

♦ "This home site is too small" is another common concern. "So, you're looking for a large yard to maintain?" can reframe this issue. Typically, prospects don't want the maintenance of a big yard. Instead, they want privacy. Reframing their objection makes the root concern apparent. If privacy is the underlying issue and the site and home selected resolve that concern, then you will probably not have to revisit the size of the home site.

♦ "The price is about $20,000 higher than we wanted to go." A common strategy for reducing or minimizing a price objection is to translate the amount into a daily expenditure, as in the following example: "On a monthly basis, $20,000 equates to about $140 monthly, or less than $5 per day, and that's prior to your tax savings."

♦ "The market is not that great right now. We're not sure it's the right time to buy a home." This objection is actually an argument for why now is a great time to buy. Explain that, as with stocks, the best time to buy a home is when prices are low, not when the market is booming.

Periodically, prospects will raise concerns that you will want to postpone responding to or perhaps not respond to at all. These issues either 1) will not prevent the prospects from moving forward, or 2) are irrelevant until the prospects determine that your offering fulfills all of their other needs. The second category of issues is major. You must address these issues before the prospects will move forward. Often, there are also individual needs that do not follow a common thread from one prospect to another. For example, a child may require a school specifically designed to work with students whose first language is not English. Although you may not be prepared immediately to deal with a concern like this, eventually you will have to. Deferring the concern until you are sure that the balance of your offering meets the prospect's needs is wise because often the prospect's desire to own your home grows and their concern will lessen over time. It also gives you time to research the issue.

The following are examples of how to defer responding to a concern:

◆ "Hmmm. That's a tough one. Why don't we come back to that if we find the right home for you, okay?"

◆ "That's interesting. Why don't we move on and if we need to spend more time on that later, we can; OK?"

◆ "I'm sorry, but I'm not sure I know what to do about that at the moment. I'll need to get back with you on that one."

Anchor

After responding to a concern, you must take an additional step before you can move forward to closing. You must use a tie-down statement to anchor a positive perspective in the prospect's mind—one that will supplant the negative concern that is causing him to resist purchasing a home. Recall how we used tie-down statements in the previous chapter to gain confirmation of the benefits of our home's features. In this context, the statement can be as simple as follows: "That resolves that, doesn't it?"

If a prospect objected to the designated high school, the dialogue for countering resistance might proceed like this:

PROSPECT: "I don't want my children going to Palmetto High School."

SALES ASSOCIATE: "I completely understand that the schools that service our community play an important role in whether Oak Trace works for you. To clarify my understanding, what is it about Palmetto High that concerns you?"

PROSPECT: "It's about four miles away and I really would prefer being within walking distance of the school."

SALES ASSOCIATE: "May I ask what your concern is associated with having your children take the bus?"

PROSPECT: "My son plays baseball and when he has practice after school he'll be too far away from home to walk and my schedule won't allow for me to pick him up regularly."

SALES ASSOCIATE: "Okay. Just to make sure I understand, you are concerned that during baseball season your son won't have transportation home after practice. Is that correct?"

PROSPECT: "Yes, that's correct."

SALES ASSOCIATE: "What grade is your son in?"

PROSPECT: "He's a junior."

SALES ASSOCIATE: "Okay, so we have a two-year issue. Is that correct?"

PROSPECT: "Yes, that's exactly right."

SALES ASSOCIATE: "So, it sounds like if we're fortunate enough to find the right home for you and your family, then we also must find a solution for your son's transportation during baseball season for the next two years. Why don't we recognize this as an unresolved issue that we'll have to readdress? I have some ideas that I can check into for you and will be happy to do so. Does that sound acceptable to you?"

PROSPECT: "Yes, that's fine for now."

School activity transportation is a major issue that must be addressed prior to moving forward. However, the issue is also irrelevant if you are not able to provide the prospect with the home they desire. Therefore, it is probably wise to defer the issue until it matters.

The following is an example of how to counter a home price objection:

PROSPECT: "The price is too high."

SALES ASSOCIATE: "Price is a major factor in such a large decision. Just to clarify my thinking, how much 'too high' do you feel it is?"

PROSPECT: "I really wanted to stay under $300,000."

SALES ASSOCIATE: "So, we're about $20,000 higher than what you had in mind; is that correct?"

PROSPECT: "Yes. I'm not comfortable with going this high."

SALES ASSOCIATE: "Okay. Not that I'm able to do this for you, but if hypothetically the price was $20,000 lower, would there be anything else preventing you from moving forward?"

PROSPECT: "No. We'd take it right now at $20,000 less."

SALES ASSOCIATE: "Unfortunately, I can't reduce the price by $20,000, but may I ask what your concern is with the price? Are you concerned about what this price does to your monthly and initial investment, or is there another concern?"

PROSPECT: "It's really about monthly payment. I was prequalified up to $300,000 and that payment was already higher than I wanted to go."

SALES ASSOCIATE: "Okay. I think I understand. So, if we were able to get your monthly and initial funds to correspond to a home priced at $300,000, would it matter to you that the home's value is actually higher?"

PROSPECT: "I'm not sure I understand."

SALES ASSOCIATE: "Many people would prefer to have a more valuable home but to have their investment in the home be more affordable. So, if I'm able to work with our lender to find you a program that will make your cash flow equivalent to what you have been prequalified for, would that resolve your issue associated with the price?"

PROSPECT: "I'm not sure. I'd have to see the program details."

SALES ASSOCIATE: "Fair enough. Why don't we make sure that we get all of the particulars associated with this home for you so that the lender has the complete picture, then we'll put them to work to find the most attractive loan program that accomplishes what you're looking for. Will that work for you?"

PROSPECT: "Yes. That sounds good."

To counter buyer resistance, identify in advance objections that prospects are likely to raise. Take time to develop responses to these concerns and develop a script that works for you using worksheet 9.1 (*see* Appendix). Use this tool to script your responses to objections. Begin by writing the objection at the top, and then complete your responses from the bottom of the worksheet up in the blank lines provided. Craft responses to the common objections listed in the "Respond" section. Then practice, drill, and rehearse. Visualize yourself executing the responses perfectly, then the next time a prospect erects an obstacle, you'll be ready to overcome it. You will find that what initially appears to be a roadblock is actually disguising a closing opportunity.

10

Closing with Confidence

losing should logically culminate a strong presentation. It should feel as natural as a happy ending to a good movie. In other words, closing is not a discrete final step but a continuous progression. It begins during the prospect's first visit to your sales office. It ends in a sale only after you have demonstrated all of the features and benefits that a location, community, home site, home, builder, and financing uniquely offer to the prospect. If you don't build increasing interest and willing participation by prospects along the way, then you will not be able to close. However, if you do engage them, then closing will feel natural and normal.

If prospects need and want your product and you don't ask them to move forward, then you are not serving them well. They may spend years in a home they don't like as well as yours because of your reluctance to close. Yet many sales associates find the most difficult area to master in sales is the closing. Any of the following 5 reasons may be causing a sales associate's difficulty:

1. Not knowing when to close
2. Ineffectively executing the other steps of the sales process

3. Not knowing how to close

4. Fearing rejection

5. Choosing not to close for fear of being a "high-pressure" salesperson

You can overcome these obstacles to closing with training and practice. So far, this book has focused mainly on giving you the tools to resolve the first two issues. The third problem requires mastering a variety of closing questions, which are explained later in this chapter. But first, let's focus on issues 4 and 5, which result from the sales associate's negative thinking.

Let's consider the possibility that you are fearful of rejection. Before you can overcome the fear, you must first recognize it. Next, realize that when prospects reject your product, they are not rejecting you. Instead, they are telling you either that your product is not what they want or that you have not convinced them that the product is right for them. Ironically, one way to avoid the feeling of personal rejection that you fear but also to ensure that your prospect rejects your product and not *you* is never to ask them to move forward with a purchase. By not asking for a sale, you might be able to avoid the temporary sting of rejection; however, you will also guarantee failure at selling.

> "What the mind can conceive and believe, the mind can achieve." [7]
>
> —NAPOLEON HILL
> *Author,* Think and Grow Rich

If you believe that asking prospects to purchase your home is pressuring them, don't beat yourself up but recognize that you need to alter this perception. Like many of us, you may have been conditioned to view sales associates through a negative lens. We have been taught to believe that sales associates are con artists who use high-pressure tactics to sell people products they don't want or need. In reality, a line separates a professional sales associate from a con artist. A con artist will harass prospects until they buy something they may not want or need, whereas a professional sales associate persuades prospects to purchase a product they really need or desire.

If you don't believe that selling homes is a worthwhile profession, you will never be happy as a sales associate. Therefore, don't let the con artists spoil your love of helping people find the home of their dreams and don't let past conditioning control your destiny. No one but you can control your actions. Selling is supposed to be fun and exciting! The sooner you internalize that belief, the sooner your sales will improve.

> "We miss 100% of the sales we don't ask for."
>
> —ZIG ZIGLAR
> *Author,* See You at the Top

New home sales professionals are educated consultants who assist people in finding solutions for the largest material transaction most will ever make. Buying a home is also the greatest emotional transaction of most people's lives—one which will impact them years into the future. You are a specialist with an awesome, unstoppable attitude. No prospect will ever experience your bad day because you know consumers are relying upon true professionals like you to assist them in a major life decision: which home to purchase.

Now that you understand your position in the home transaction, I want to teach you the specifics of closing. There are two general types of closing questions: trial closing and closing. Trial closing questions are simply questions that, when answered, will tell you how close the prospect is to making a purchase decision and, therefore, what you should do next. Trial closing questions tend to ask the prospect for opinions, whereas closing questions require the prospect to make decisions.

Trial Closing Questions

Trial closing questions are an essential and easy-to-incorporate element of presentations. When prospects respond to them with their opinions, you can move forward regardless of what those opinions are. Opinions aren't right or wrong; they're simply the feedback you need to stay on course. People like to opine. Trial closing questions will engage your prospects in a nonthreatening way. These questions can be based in reality or they can be hypothetical.

Reality Based

The following are examples of reality-based trial closing questions:

◆ "Susan, from what you've seen of the Nottingham so far, what do you think about it?"

- "Susan, how do you feel about the Nottingham from what you've seen so far?"
- "What's your feeling, Susan? Would you prefer to have the corner site or the oversized site on the cul-de-sac?"
- "What do you think you'd use this room for?"
- "Do you think you'd want a fireplace in this room?"
- "How do you think you'd place your furniture in this room?"
- "Susan, do you think you'd prefer a home that is already under construction or is a six-month building time acceptable?"
- "Susan, from what you've seen so far of the community, how do you feel about it?"
- "We feature wood flooring in this home but offer many different options. Have you considered what you'd want in your home?"
- "In your opinion, Susan, how does the Nottingham compare to the other homes you've seen?"
- "Would this be something you'd want in your home, Susan?"
- "How do you like this bonus room?"

Hypothetical

The following are examples of hypothetical trial closing questions:

- "How soon would you plan on moving after you found the right home?"
- "If you were to decide on the Nottingham, would the three- or four-bedroom plan best suit your needs?"
- "Would you want the two- or three-car garage if you were to decide to move forward?"
- "Susan, if price was not a factor, would you prefer the Nottingham or the Pinehurst?"
- "If you were to decide on the Nottingham, what options do you think you'd like to have?"
- "I mentioned that we have three exterior designs for each plan. Do you like this one or do you think you'd like to see the others?"
- "I mentioned that we have three exterior designs for each plan. How does this one feel to you?"
- "Would the game room be something you'd include if you were to decide on this home?"

If the steps leading to the final closing are sound, and your trial closes have given you the feedback that you have the home that suits their needs, then closing should not be difficult. If you still find closing uncomfortable, then examine your presentation. It may have weak points that you can strengthen with some thought and practice.

Closing Questions

Following are 15 types of closing questions that address the 6 areas of a home purchase:

Education

The education close allows you to ask a question that, when answered, will allow you to educate the prospect about process while moving them closer to a decision. Here is an example:

> "Have you had an opportunity to talk to a lender in order to understand the monthly and initial investment required for a home in this price range?"

Request to Move Forward

This close should only occur when you believe you have addressed all of the decisions necessary for the prospect to move forward. Once you have, you can use the following questions to ease a prospect forward:

- "Is there any reason why we can't move forward?"
- "Is there something that I have not fully explained that needs to be addressed in order for you to move ahead today?"
- "Is there anything that we need to address before moving forward?"

Alternative Choice

In this closing scenario, you offer prospects choices in which any answer moves them forward, as in the following example: "We have two sites remaining that will accommodate this home plan. Would you prefer the site that offers the security of neighbors all around you or the more private site backing to the conservation area?"

Summary

The summary allows you to review all decisions the prospects have made and allows you to clarify what they really want. Therefore, it potentially transitions naturally to a final decision to move forward. When the prospects answer the question, they are basically agreeing with all of the other aspects of the transaction you have summarized. Consider the following example:

> "If I understand correctly, you like the Longboat 4-bedroom plan especially because of the loft and upstairs space; you prefer home site 121 because of the conservation view and privacy; and you agreed that you prefer the garage on the right so that your lanai opens up to the lake. And which exterior design was it that you liked the best?"

Assumptive

The assumptive close assumes the prospect has already decided to move forward. You are now merely finalizing the details associated with the transaction, as in the following examples:

- "Let me show you what the financing looks like."
- "I'll be happy to schedule your appointment with the lender and design center. What does your schedule look like next week?"
- "Would you like to browse some of the cabinet selections while I get started putting this together?"
- "If you'll OK this paperwork, we can reserve the site today."

Last Chance

The last chance close creates a sense of urgency while communicating a benefit of buying now. Prospects tend to prefer getting one of the last opportunities. The following is a last chance closing question:

"As you know, we only have two more opportunities available prior to our next price increase. Do you want one of them?"

Exclusive Opportunity

Most prospects want the home they decide to purchase to be unique—not something that anyone and everyone can have. Providing something that is special for an elite few can often make the difference between selling a home or not. Therefore, point out the unique features of the home, community, and location, as in the following example:

"I'm not aware of any new home offering that provides . . . . It seems to be just what you're looking for. Don't you agree?"

Follow the Leader

Although people want unique features in their homes, they also like a "deal" and want the same thing, or better, than what their neighbors have. If others believe that you are offering an exceptional value, then your prospects are likely to believe this as well. No one wants to live in a community that others don't want to live in. The following is an example of a follow-the-leader closing question:

"Silver Lake is such an exceptional opportunity. We have over 40 families that have already decided to make Silver Lake their home. Do you want to be next?"

Yes

In the yes close, you build up to asking prospects to close on a home by first asking them a series of questions to which you know their answers will be "yes." The theory is that if you ask enough questions the prospect will say yes to, then they will say yes to closing on the home as well. Consider the following example:

"Let me review what we have decided so far. You like the location of the community as it relates to your work, correct? You said the community amenities, entryway, and landscaping really look pristine, right? And we selected what I think you believe is the best remaining home site offering you the view and the privacy you desire; isn't that right? And I know you adore the home, don't you? Then is there any reason why we can't get started with the paper work?"

The Ask

Perhaps the most direct and straightforward approach, the ask requests prospects to decide to buy. Here is an example:

- "Let's go back to the office and I'll show you what we'll need to do to get started, OK?"
- "If you think this may be the site for you, why don't you reserve it?"
- "Do you see any major issues we might have to address in order to reserve this site for you?"
- "Is this the site you prefer?"

Ben Franklin

Benjamin Franklin is said to have used a "balance sheet" to make decisions. You can apply his technique to closing on a home sale like this:

"As you know, Americans have long considered Benjamin Franklin one of our wisest men. Whenever he was in a situation like you're in today, he felt pretty much as you do about it. If it was the right thing to do, he wanted to be sure he did it. If it was the wrong thing, he wanted to be sure to avoid it. Isn't that pretty much the same way you feel?

"Well, here's what he used to do. He'd take a sheet of paper and draw a line down the middle. At the top of the first column, he'd write 'Yes,' and then list all the reasons to move forward with the decision. On the second column, he'd write 'No,' and list all the reasons against the decision. When he was finished, he counted the reasons listed in each column and made a decision based on the numbers. Why don't we give it a try?"

You would continue by listing pros and cons, freely assisting the prospect in identifying reasons to move forward, but not reasons against a purchase.

Think It Over

Many prospects say they want to "think it over" to delay making a decision. Don't be surprised if prospects try to stall making a final decision once all of the other decisions regarding location, community, home site, home, builder, and financing have been made. They may feel pressured and want time to digest everything. You can ease their anxiety as follows:

> "I think that's a good idea. I certainly wouldn't want you to move forward and later have regrets. But just to clarify my thinking, can you share with me exactly what you need to think about? You did really love the home plan, didn't you?"

List and gain confirmation on all of the things you know they like about your offering. Then ask, "Can you level with me? Could it possibly be the price?"

Reduce It

In the context of closing, reduce it means simplifying the price, not offering to discount it. As discussed previously, the best way to handle a price objection is to reduce the cost of owning the home to a daily expenditure, as in the following examples:

- "So, if I understand correctly, the price is about $5,000 more than what you had in mind. Is that correct? I'm not sure if you realize this, but $5,000 equates to about $35 per month and that is pretax. I would guess it's less than $30 a month, after tax, which means we're talking about $1 a day to have exactly what you're looking for."
- "Just to put things in perspective, are you going to decide to go elsewhere and live the next several years in a home you don't like as well as this one for less than the cost of a daily cup of coffee?"

Suggestion

Suggestions are easily accepted by prospects. Therefore, you should make many suggestions throughout your presentation. By doing so, you close the prospect on the next step in the buying process as the following example demonstrates:

> "Let me make a suggestion. Why don't we take a look at the neighborhood layout and see which sites could accommodate this plan?"

Porcupine

The porcupine closing technique is so named because when prospects raise an objection you immediately toss it back as the reason for them to move forward. For example, if your prospect says the housing market is weak so he doesn't want to move forward, your response could be as follows:

> "That is exactly why you should consider moving forward. When the market is good, it typically means that there is more demand than supply, and in that scenario, prices escalate. Now, however, you are certain to get a good value and ultimately that should result in greater appreciation in the long run. That makes sense, doesn't it?"

Keep Practicing

If you were surprised to learn that there are 15 different types of closes, think about this: Most sales trainers, including me, believe that you will need to attempt a final close 3 to 5 times before concluding a real estate transaction. You must familiarize yourself with and become comfortable using all 15 types in order to assist your prospects and to be among the best sales professionals in the industry. Pick at least 5 of these closings and memorize them, role-play them, and internalize them. They will become natural and instinctive. When the opportunity arises, you will have the words you need to smoothly and effectively close the transaction.

11

Financing 101

If you are selling homes at comparatively lower price points than competitors in your area, you must understand the basics of financing and the advantages of owning rather than renting. As with prospecting, don't delude yourself that financing is someone else's responsibility. Whenever you allow prospects to leave your sales office without resolving their issue, you increase the risk of losing a sale. By resolving a prospect's concern without sending the person elsewhere and lengthening their home search, you are adding value and increasing your chances of success.

Learn to quickly calculate monthly principal, interest, taxes, and insurance (PITI) and the initial investment to own one of your homes. To do this, you must keep abreast of interest rate changes, terms, and lending programs. At a minimum, review these items weekly. If you notice that the market is changing more rapidly than that, make time to review the lending environment more frequently. You must fully understand available financing alternatives because the quality of prospects depends on their ability to finance a home. Lenders consider prospects' available cash, credit history, and their ongoing cash flow when qualifying them for loans.

Credit

Generally, the prospect's credit history greatly influences the type of loan they can get. Lenders look at prospects' credit scores from the various credit reporting agencies. Loan applicants with scores in the upper 700s are considered to be excellent credit risks. If your prospects' credit and other criteria are very good, they can probably get terms more favorable than those on a conforming loan. Conforming loans are those that can be sold on the secondary market to government-sponsored enterprises Fannie Mae and Freddie Mac. These loans have an automated approval process, which means that the loan officer enters applicants' data into a software program and if the applicants meet the underwriting guidelines, they are approved without human intervention. (The applicants must eventually provide proper documentation.)

Scores of 620 to 700 are considered average. Lenders typically approve prospects with average credit scores for conforming loans; however, interest on these loans may not be at the current market rate, depending upon the ratio of the loan amount to the home's value. Prospects with scores under 620 typically do not get the current market rate, even with a lower loan-to-value ratio, and other terms also may be less desirable. With changes in the lending market in 2008 and 2009, applicants that could not obtain a conforming loan had very few options. However, lending guidelines change rapidly based upon current economic conditions and those conditions always improve eventually.

In the past, high-risk applicants often could qualify with nonconforming lenders. Because these lenders do not sell outstanding loans to Fannie Mae and Freddie Mac, they can approve loans to borrowers who do not conform to Fannie and Freddie's guidelines. Although high-risk borrowers may have difficulty getting any mortgage financing during a particular period, credit availability, like economic conditions, is fluid. As a sales associate, you must stay abreast of current financing trends, which can significantly impact your sales results.

Interest Rates

Market rate is the interest rate that creditors assign to most loans on the secondary market. If a loan to a high-risk borrower is not considered salable on the secondary market, some lenders still will lend the money. However, these high-risk loans come with less desirable terms that usually include significantly higher interest rates.

In both instances—loans to very low-risk borrowers and to high-risk borrowers—lenders often issue financing because they can carry the loan to maturity. They are portfolio loans, meaning the lender is keeping them within its own portfolio of liabilities.

Calculating Debt Ratios

Cash flow stability indicates whether the borrower has a track record of incoming cash that can support the new mortgage payment. Conforming loans assess this by analyzing debt-to-income ratios. Underwriters frequently examine two types of ratios: housing debt to gross income and long-term debt to income. For conforming loans, borrowers may use up to 28% of their monthly gross income to pay for housing expenses. To calculate the percentage, use the following formula:

$$\frac{\text{PITI}}{\text{Monthly Gross Income}}$$

The borrower's total long-term debt-to-income ratio for conforming loans may be more than one-third of their monthly gross income. Long-term debt includes alimony, child support, credit card debt, and other loan payments due. It does not include living expenses such as utility bills. You can calculate the ratio using the following formula:

$$\frac{\text{PITI} + \text{Total Monthly Debt}}{\text{Monthly Gross Income}}$$

FHA Loans

The Federal Housing Administration (FHA) is a government entity established to encourage homeownership by requiring homes to meet minimum standards and by creating financing options with lower down payments. FHA guarantees a loan as long as it meets specific criteria, thereby allowing lenders to issue loans with lower down payments and higher income-to-debt ratios than those for conforming loans, without the corresponding financial risk. FHA's housing-to-debt ratio is 29% and total debt-to-income ratio is 41%. FHA's maximum loan limit varies by area home prices.

VA Loans

The Veterans Administration (VA) offers a guaranteed loan benefit for U.S. military veterans. A veteran receives a certificate of eligibility informing lenders how much the veteran is eligible to borrow under the guarantee program. The VA home loan ratio combines the PITI and all other long-term debt into a single debt-to-income ratio of 41%. If an eligible veteran has no other debt, he or she can borrow more under the VA program than under any other loan program. However, VA does have a maximum loan limit that is periodically updated. Therefore, you must know the current limit, which can be found at the United States Department of Veterans Affairs Web site: http://www.homeloans.va.gov. In most cases, if the borrower has excellent credit, the ratios may be more flexible. With poor credit, the ratios are more rigid.

Loan Terms

If borrowers could pay cash for a home (even if they don't), ratios and credit scores become less important to lenders. Lenders consider available cash and net worth when deciding whether or not to approve a loan.

Conforming loans usually require the borrower to have adequate funds to close on the loan plus two months of mortgage payments. FHA and VA loans require one month of reserves. Under all programs—conforming, FHA, and VA—different types of loans exist, including the following:

- 15-, 20-, 30-, and 40-year terms
- fixed interest rates
- adjustable interest rates
- first and second loan programs
- interest-only loans
- 100% financing

Thirty-year terms are the most common. Longer terms are available but not common when credit is tight. Fixed-rate programs are geared toward borrowers who expect to be in their homes for many years. Sometimes the difference between fixed- and adjustable-rate programs are not significant. Therefore, even those who intend to be in their homes for only a few years may want a fixed interest rate.

There are several types of adjustable-rate programs. The 3/1, 5/1, and 7/1 adjustable-rate mortgage (ARM) programs are good options for those who intend to be in their homes for fewer than 7 years. A 3/1 ARM offers a fixed rate for 3 years, usually at a lower rate than a fixed-rate loan or the 5/1 or 7/1 ARMs. However, after 3 years, the loan adjusts annually. Usually, the longer the initial fixed-rate of the ARM, the higher the rate eventually becomes.

Home buyers can often benefit by applying two different loans to a home purchase. The first loan is typically for 80% of the home's appraised value and the second loan is for 10 to 15%. This strategy typically allows the borrower a combined payment lower than a conforming 90 to 95% loan because there is no mortgage insurance premium. (Loans for which the borrower contributes a down payment of less than 20% typically require the buyer to purchase private mortgage insurance or PMI.)

Interest-only financing allows borrowers to pay only the interest on the loan instead of paying off principal. The principal is not paid until the loan matures. This option became popular in markets with high and escalating real estate values during the last housing boom. These loans help keep monthly payments as low as possible, and monthly payments on more traditional financing typically don't make a significant dent in principal until well into the loan term anyway. Nevertheless, financing 100% of a home's value has become difficult and, in fact, may become obsolete.

Price vs. Cost

When discussing financing with prospects, you must be able to calculate an estimated PITI payment in order to illustrate the financial benefits of homeownership. If your company's prospect management software does not include a mortgage calculator you should consider obtaining a financial calculator and having your favorite loan officer instruct you on how to use it. Readers who are savvy with Excel can develop a spreadsheet for this purpose. In addition, many Web sites offer mortgage calculators, including Yahoo! Finance at http://finance.yahoo.com/calculator/family home/hom03. This calculator allows you to play with a variety of scenarios. You do not have to provide contact information to use it as you must with some calculator pages hosted by specific lending institutions.

Here's an example of why knowledge of home financing is a valuable sales tool: A $2,008 monthly payment on a $200,000 home includes approximately $1,235 in interest, all of which is tax deductible. If your prospect is in a 30% tax bracket, he will save $370 per month in income taxes.

In addition, homes usually appreciate in value. Assuming a modest 3% annual appreciation over 5 years, the home owners would gain approximately $31,850 in home value. If they chose to sell the home after that, their net gain would be about $13,300 after deducting 8% of the home's sales price for selling expenses. That profit would equate to $220 per month during the 5 years the owners are in the home. Their cost of homeownership then, is reduced to less than $1,500 per month: $2,008 – $370 – $220 = $1,418.

Show prospects the difference between price and cost. Although the home price may be $200,000, the monthly cost of ownership is much lower than most people realize. Showing prospects the difference between price and cost may provide the incentive they need to move forward with a purchase. Therefore, this calculation is the minimum that a professional sales associate must be able to perform for his or her prospects.

12

Knowing Your Competition

*M*any sales associates allow their companies to set home prices and then either accept the prices or complain about them. At the same time, many home builders, unfortunately, establish prices based on profit expectations rather than on what the market will bear. A more productive approach to selling is to team with your builder proactively to ensure that your company prices homes competitively for your market. Whether your builder's priority is sales velocity or profit margin, you can become a valuable partner in determining an appropriate pricing strategy. As a sales associate, you benefit from knowing exactly what the local market will allow you to charge for a home and the number of sales to expect according to home price.

Competitors are a key source of market intelligence. Therefore, sales associates should shop other new home communities regularly for information about pricing, product, prospects, and selling strategies. First, determine who your competitors are. Unless your homes or communities are unique and present a "one of a kind" offering without any competition, which most do not, your competition will be located in your immediate surrounding area. In a few cases, however, builders in other states or even in other countries may be competing for your buyers. However, most builders' competition is within a few miles of their sales office.

Keep in mind when shopping your competition that today's homes are commodities with designs that are easily and frequently copied. Therefore, you must gather details about competitors that will allow you to set your offering apart and offer prospects something unique to your market— something that your competitors are not offering. The following is the bare minimum of information you should learn about your competitors:

> **The price of the homes** being offered, including the current incentive programs, if any.
>
> **The home plans.** Obtain the home plans for all of the homes offered in the neighborhoods, including any bonus or flexible space options available with each design.
>
> **The buyer demographics,** including age, family status, and income. This information doesn't have to be exact and can often be observed simply by driving through the neighborhood. What types of cars are prospects driving? Who would the amenities appeal to? Who are the existing home owners in the community?
>
> **The psychographics** of the current home owners, including customers' motivations for buying. In some cases, this is easy to assess. For example, if you observe that the community is a first-time home buyer community, then the buyers' motivation is often related to improving their standard of living. They usually buy as a result of marriage or because they are expecting a child. Sometimes you cannot easily assess who the buyers are, especially in a first or second move-up community. If the sales associate is cooperative, he or she may share with you information such as where most prospects are moving from and what is prompting them to move to the community versus competitors'.

There is no substitute for gathering this information firsthand. Visiting new home communities in person allows you to observe the intangibles of a great or average community that go beyond home designs and prices. This observation will help you to differentiate your homes and community. As you visit communities, gather the following information:

A complete brochure, which should include

- price list
- home plans
- neighborhood layout
- list of included features

A list of the home site premiums. This information isn't often in a written format designed to give to prospects. You may have to get the prices from the sales associates while they show you the neighborhood layout. You may ask them the site premiums of a few sites and gather enough information to be beneficial to your analysis of their offering.

Net sales during the past 90 days. You can ask the sales associate for this figure, but you may not get accurate information. You can verify a competitor's sales volume by looking at publicly available information on building permits and the number of homes the community has under construction. For example, if the permitting time is 30 days and it takes approximately 60 days to get to the framing stage of construction, you can simply count the number of homes under construction that are at the frame stage or earlier. This would represent two months of sales and you can estimate the third month to be similar. Subtract the number of inventory starts, which you can usually easily obtain from the sales associate on-site. Feel free to ask the construction superintendent about sales if you run into him or her. I have found that the superintendent will provide accurate information about sales and inventory.

The two most popular home plans. The sales associate will often provide this information or you can identify the most popular plans by driving through the neighborhood and looking at which plans are under construction. Most of the time, you will find the models are the most popular plans. However, if you see a popular plan that is not modeled, make sure to compare the plan to your builder's offerings. A bestselling plan that is not modeled is probably exceptional, and your company would likely want to sell something comparable.

The typical home site size. The majority of the home sites in a community meet a minimum size, are rectangular in shape, and accommodate most of the builder's home plans.

Whether or not closing costs are paid. The amount may vary depending on whether borrowers use a preferred lender or their own lender. Find out how much is contributed in each scenario.

Current incentives the builder is offering to buyers, including interest rate buy-downs, free options, paid closing costs, discounts on home site premiums, or base-price incentives.

Features of the competitor's product, community, and location that are not offered in your community. Compare all of these items to your offering and make note of items included in your competitor's base-price home. Also, consider optional items that you are not able to offer.

Features missing from the competitor's community that your community offers. Compare your community features and make note of those items you offer that are not available in your competitor's community.

The builder's negotiation philosophy. Do they negotiate and reduce their base price? Will they provide some options at no charge? What about reducing site premiums or not charging for these extras at all? What are the terms? Will the builder accept home-to-sell contingencies or set up a payment plan to save for a down payment? If the sales associate is not forthcoming with this information, a Realtor or prospect can often get it for you. Another alternative is to hire a professional shopper to get the information.

The builder's policies about Realtors. Does the builder offer commissions? Bonuses? Incentives? What are the requirements when registering a prospect? Can a Realtor phone register? Must the Realtor accompany prospects on their first visit or is any time prior to the sale acceptable?

Home owners' association (HOA) dues and community development district fees. What are the costs? When are they collected? What do they include?

The sales associate's ability. A strong sales associate can make a weak community more competitive than the rest of the analysis will show.

Any other material difference between you and your competitor. Some differences—such as schools, proximity to major thoroughfares, visual traffic window, and many others—are intangibles but materially affect the value of an offering.

Worksheet 12.1 (*see* Appendix) was designed to help you gather market intelligence.

Compare the Homes

The information can be entered into an Excel spreadsheet and then graphed to compare your community with your competitor's. Your builder's

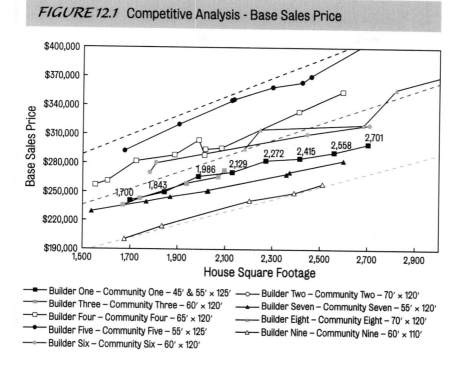

FIGURE 12.1 Competitive Analysis - Base Sales Price

- ▬■▬ Builder One – Community One – 45′ & 55′ × 125′
- ▬▬ Builder Three – Community Three – 60′ × 120′
- ▬□▬ Builder Four – Community Four – 65′ × 120′
- ▬●▬ Builder Five – Community Five – 55′ × 125′
- ▬●▬ Builder Six – Community Six – 60′ × 120′
- ▬○▬ Builder Two – Community Two – 70′ × 120′
- ▬▲▬ Builder Seven – Community Seven – 55′ × 120′
- ▬▬ Builder Eight – Community Eight – 70′ × 120′
- ▬△▬ Builder Nine – Community Nine – 60′ × 110′

vice president of sales and marketing or finance can probably do this for you if you don't know how to do it.

Have the data graphed two ways. In the first graph, place your base prices on the Y (vertical) axis and the square footage of your homes on the X (horizontal) axis (fig. 12.1). This graph will allow you to compare your base prices to your competition's to see whether your community is likely to remain a contender after prospects make their first-round eliminations discussed earlier in this book. If your base prices are high compared with communities that offer similar features, you probably won't survive consumers' first cut.

The dashed lines at the top and bottom of the graph show the range of pricing that you can see on the Y axis to the left. In this graph, the price range is from $190,000 to $400,000. The dashed line in the center represents a midpoint. The solid data series that shows the square footage of each home next to each data point represents the subject property, or in this case, my community. As a general rule, the offering should appear below the midpoint pricing line, which keeps your base pricing in the bot-

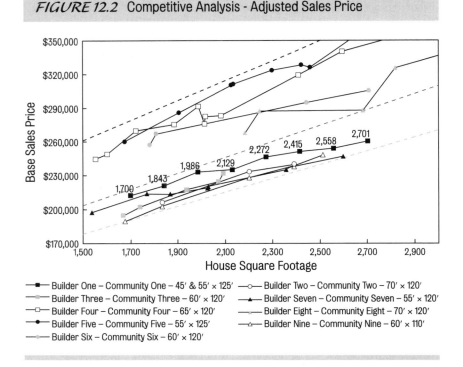

FIGURE 12.2 Competitive Analysis - Adjusted Sales Price

— Builder One – Community One – 45' & 55' × 125'   —o— Builder Two – Community Two – 70' × 120'
— Builder Three – Community Three – 60' × 120'   —▲— Builder Seven – Community Seven – 55' × 120'
—□— Builder Four – Community Four – 65' × 120'   — Builder Eight – Community Eight – 70' × 120'
—•— Builder Five – Community Five – 55' × 125'   —△— Builder Nine – Community Nine – 60' × 110'
— Builder Six – Community Six – 60' × 120'

tom half of what is available to the prospect. It will probably keep you from being eliminated because of price.

The second graph is a scatter graph that considers both home and community features (fig. 12.2). Your home and community features represent the baseline, and all of your competition's prices are adjusted to fit your specifications. Figure 12.3 illustrates that the baseline is a single-family home with 2 baths and a 2-car garage. Prices for plans in comparison communities are adjusted to be comparable to a 2-bath, 2-car-garage plan.

For example, if your competitor has a plan with a 3-car garage and if the approximate market value of a 3-car garage versus a 2-car garage is $10,000, then the plan with the 3-car garage would be worth $10,000 more than the 2-car garage. If your competitor has a community or plan feature that is superior to that which you offer, you increase the competitor's plan by making a positive adjustment equivalent to the market value of that superior feature. In other words, if the home buyer must purchase an option from you that is included with your competitor's offering, you reduce the

FIGURE 12.3 Community Market Analysis - Competing Community Detail

Builder Two:	Creation Communities				**Subdivision**	Oak Trace	
Lot Size:	70' x120'	**Total Sites:**	143	**Avail Sites:**	62	**Total Sales:**	81

Critical Community Factors:

Creation Communities has a very impressive entry. Really catches the eye. Home sites in Oak Trace are either on water view or conservation. Also has desirable amenities that include ftness center, clubhouse, pool, and walking trails.

Plan Name (* - If a Model)		Denison	Destin	Desoto	
Stories/Bedrooms/Baths/Garage		1/3/2/2	1/4/2/2	2/4/2.5/2	
House Sq. Ft.		1,834	2,202	2,390	
Base Sales Price		**$213,900**	**$240,900**	**$249,400**	
Price/Sq. Ft.		$116.63	$109.40	$104.35	
Adjustments:					
half bath	($2,000)			($2,000)	
smooth surface range	($250)	($250)	($250)	($250)	
above range microwave	($750)	($750)	($750)	($750)	
amenities	($2,000)	($2,000)	($2,000)	($2,000)	
blinds (front only)	($1,000)	($1,000)	($1,000)	($1,000)	
security system	($800)	($800)	($800)	($800)	
garage opener pre-wire	($150)	($150)	($150)	($150)	
location	($2,500)	($2,500)	($2,500)	($2,500)	
site differential	($4,000)	($4,000)	($4,000)	($4,000)	
exterior coach light (1)	($150)	($150)	($150)	($150)	
tile in all wet areas	($3,000)	($3,000)	($3,000)	($3,000)	
Financing			$0	$0	$0	
Total Adjustment		($12,600)	($12,600)	($14,600)	
Adjusted Sales Price		**$201,300**	**$228,300**	**$234,800**	
Price/Sq. Ft.		$109.76	$103.68	$98.24	

Product Standard Feature Analysis:

Creation Communities has more included features which would typically be optional in our neighborhood. However, we believe that Creation Communities has overpriced the market because of this and that the target market is more fnancially conscious.

Product Specification Difference Analysis:

The building specifications are similar to our offering without any significant differences.

Buyer Financing Analysis and Other Comments/Notes:

3% to Realtors. CDD fees of $2,000-$2,200 annually. $10,000 incentive on inventories, $6,000 on To Be Built. Average incentive noted above.

competitor's offering. If the home buyer must purchase a feature in your competitor's home that is included in your base price, then you increase the competitor's offering. This way, you can compare apples to apples.

Talk to Your Builder

These graphs provide builders with the data to make informed decisions about price or plan adjustments, if necessary, based on a home's market value rather than on the cost of providing a particular feature. With this information, a builder can determine prices and project sales volume. As a sales associate, you can use these tools to discuss possible price adjustments with the builder. If your builder is expecting to average the same sales volume for your neighborhood as the competitor's but your neighborhood appears in the upper third of the adjusted graph, the builder's expectations may be unrealistic.

For example, the price difference for a given site, as noted in the table, is based on its perceived value rather than on the actual cost associated with the larger site. When adjustments are made, builders should base them on the market value, not the builder's cost. Ultimately, what does a prospect believe an item is worth? A garage with room for a third car, for example, is not as valuable in a first-time home buyer market as in a move-up buyer market. Adjust prices based on a given situation. What is the prospect willing to pay to get the item included? The answer to that question is the amount you should use for each adjustment.

The middle dashed line on figure 12.2 splits the graph to show the bottom third of the price range. The subject property is the solid dark data series in which the square footage of each home design appears next to each data point.

To achieve average absorption or sales volume compared with its competitors, a community should be on the bottom half of the base price graph and on the bottom third of the adjusted price graph. Therefore, if you want higher-than-average sales velocity compared with your competitors, you must adjust prices to position your community lower on the graphs. Conversely, if your builder wants to achieve higher margins while selling less volume, your community should be positioned higher on the graph.

The graphs also can be used as a tool to gauge your personal performance. If your sales are outpacing the market yet your graphs show your homes are in the middle of the pack, you can feel great about the value you are adding to your builder's bottom line. Share this information with your builder.

Adjust Your Presentations

You also can use these tools to inform your presentations to prospects. You will know you are making the most of your home's features by demonstrating those that are superior to your competitors'. Without knowing the details of what your competition offers, your model home demonstration may neglect to address features that add value to your offering compared with that of your competition.

Although the ability and quality of the sales associate significantly impacts overall sales results, we do not include this information in the graph. Simply put, most companies determine their plan for the future based on a typical sales associate rather than a superstar. Therefore, if you work at becoming a sales associate who consistently outperforms your competition, you will add significantly to your builder's profits and companies will tend to reward you accordingly.

Conclusion

*M*idway through writing this book, I got a call that had nothing to do with home sales but which would eventually reaffirm my belief in the power of "it" in determining the course of one's personal and professional achievements— or lack thereof. The call was from an associate who asked if I would be interested in running a marathon with her. I had run a couple of 5Ks before, but 26.2 miles? Although I didn't say it, I was thinking that my friend must be crazy. But after I learned that the marathon was to bene- fit the Leukemia & Lymphoma Society, one of the charities I am most committed to, I readily agreed to do it. I really didn't understand what I was getting into.

Now let me tell you about my bionic right leg. I tore my plantar fas- cia, located in the arch of the foot, running a 5K race, and broke my tibia and my fibula (lower leg bones) playing softball. I have a plate, four screws, and a pin in my leg as a result of the latter injury. I tore my lateral collateral knee ligament while skiing, and my pelvis was fractured in an auto accident. Somehow I neglected to consider any of these injuries when I committed to running a marathon.

During the 4½ months of training, I had several setbacks, including a pulled hamstring, and was out for 3 weeks. To maintain my cardio-vascular strength, I began swimming. Then, I caught pneumonia, which took me away from my training schedule for almost 2 weeks.

My bad knee gave me ongoing challenges and required that I run on soft surfaces. I learned this fact only after running about 15 miles on concrete, which took me out of training for the next 4 days. To top it all off, a week before the race I woke up with a 103° temperature and a sore throat. Six days prior to my marathon, I visited a doctor, who told me I had strep throat. I told him I was running a marathon in 6 days and needed advice about the most expeditious way to recover. He told me not to run the marathon. So I restated my question: "I am running a marathon on Sunday. Knowing that, now what advice would you give?"

The following Sunday morning at 1 a.m. I woke up after 7 hours of sleep in my Orlando, Florida, hotel room to get ready for a 2:15 a.m. breakfast with the team I had been training with. At 3:00 a.m. we took a bus from our hotel to the event. The race was scheduled to begin at 5:50 a.m., and the five of us who had been training together were all there and ready to go.

What made me think that at my age, with all my injuries and setbacks and not even fully recovered from strep throat, that I could even finish this race? I never believed that failure was an option.

During my training, the longest distance I had run was 18 miles. So, I would have to go 8.2 additional miles to complete the race. I remember thinking at mile 9 that I was feeling really good and I knew I could go the distance. But by mile 15, my quadriceps, right knee, and left foot were killing me. Still more than 10 miles from finishing the race, I had a choice to make. I could believe that because of all of my injuries and setbacks during training, it was acceptable not to finish the race. I could have used those things as excuses to justify failure. Or, I could choose to begin to work on my thoughts and my self-talk to ensure that I would finish.

I remember thinking, when I was training and was in pain, that it was wise to stop running because I had to continue to train the next day, and if I pushed myself too much, I might have another setback and not be able to recover in time for the race. But running the marathon was different because after this race, I wouldn't have to train again. When tomorrow came, it would be OK if my muscles ached; I could deal with the pain. The joy of accomplishing the goal was much more important to me. "I must create success habits, not failure habits," I said to myself. "Quitting would just be an example of failure, not success."

Eventually, I was able to focus on the joy of the marathon and not the pain. The pain was there, but it wasn't my focus, and the joy of crossing the finish line for such a worthy cause would be far more lasting that any pain I was enduring, I told myself. I convinced myself that finishing would give me wonderful memories for years to come.

Ultimately, thanks to Biofreeze and, more importantly, mind over matter, by mile 20, something came over me and I was able to block out the pain entirely. Time began to fly by. I think this was the first time I actually achieved the "runner's high" I had heard about. I was in a state of bliss where each mile seemed easier than the prior one. It was an amazing feeling. My last mile was probably the fastest of the entire race.

After passing the finish line, all I could think about was I should just keep running because if I stopped, I might be in too much pain to walk. I ran almost the entire distance back to the sign-out area. I was so sore but so happy even though, as I suspected it might be, walking was a challenge afterward.

I tell you this story not for my own glorification but to encourage you to press on when it seems impossible to keep going. When the market is slow, or when you face negative situations in your career, your willpower and resolve must be the strongest. During these tough times, when you succeed, your success will feel even more wondrous. It is up to you. You decide your success or failure at every given moment. You can focus on the poor market or the bad location of your community or myriad other things that prevent you from attaining the success you desire. But when you focus on the pain, and not the result you want, you only help the pain to be realized.

They say that running a marathon is 90% mental. I say that success in new homes sales is 90% mental. If you master your thoughts and shape your beliefs properly, every possible success is yours.

Not only do you have to have "it," you must also practice executing the perfect sale and continue to deepen your understanding of people and their buying process.

Keep in mind that before prospects enter your sales office they are one-third of the way through their buying process. This means your offering has already made a positive impression that kept you in the race. Whether the prospects found you because of your prospecting efforts or your company's marketing efforts, more than 80% of them will have visited your company Web site and drawn some conclusions about your offering before their first visit. Identifying those conclusions is beneficial to your success and will allow you to find a solution to your prospects' needs more efficiently.

Understanding your prospects' motivational and behavior patterns is also critical to your success. Consider the platinum rule: Do unto others as they wish to be done unto. Whether you're dealing with an authority figure, a center of attention, a social club member, or a bean counter, alter your style to fit their personality. Recognize that you must communicate differently with visual, kinesthetic, and auditory prospects and that prospects' body language communicates different emotions as well. Your ability to become a master at understanding what is *not* being said will contribute greatly to your success. Understanding how to read and communicate with prospects and to take into consideration their different personality styles and sensory dominance is actually more difficult than learning sales techniques but it is more powerful in building rapport. Your goal in the gallery is to build rapport and close on being able to demonstrate your model homes with the prospect.

Successful model home demonstrations are planned; they do not just occur by accident. Shop your competition regularly for information that will allow you to sell to your prospects the features and benefits you offer that your competitors do not, and educate your builder, if necessary, about the competitiveness of your offering.

Map the flow of your model home demonstrations on a home plan. Write a feature/bridge/benefit/tie-down statement for every feature you intend to demonstrate and develop the qualifying questions you are going to ask in each area. Practice your opening statements, transitions, and trial closes for each demonstration area.

Remember to apply the five-step process to overcome resistance and regularly close along the way. Then, move forward naturally and with ease. Your final closing question is simply the last scene before the happy ending to the buyer's home search story.

Don't forget about financing the home. The financing landscape is ever-changing and your prospects turn to you to understand what they can afford. Make sure that you spend time with a trusted loan officer so you understand current financing trends. Your knowledge of financing can determine whether or not you are able to move forward with your prospects today.

Picture the perfect presentation that starts with your greeting, gallery presentation, and model home demonstration. You have mastered rapport by understanding the different personality and sensory dominance preferences. You have developed an exceptional use of words that are empowering and help you advance the sale. You build in qualifying questions and aptly discuss features and benefits. Along the way, you overcome resistance and use trial closes to better understand prospects' needs and find the solution to their desired location, community, home site, home, builder, and financing. Then you smoothly and easily close with confidence knowing that your offering is perfect for them. You have become the true professional that you have dreamed of. You have "it"!

As I finish this book, it is a Wednesday afternoon. There is nothing special about this Wednesday except that it follows the very special Sunday when I ran my first marathon. What made that Sunday special was not a mile marker but the clear proof that mental power—mind over matter—will change the outcome.

If you are not achieving the results that you would like, then it's time for you to begin to think differently and put your thoughts into action. Commit to making change happen in your life by adopting constructive beliefs and behaviors.

You are the master of your destiny. Mastery means "great skillfulness and knowledge of some subject or activity." However, if you continue to think and act as you have in the past, no amount of knowledge will change your results. Success starts with you and ends with you. Blaming anyone or anything else—including your builder or the market—for your circumstances is just an excuse to avoid changing. By focusing on the person you want to become rather than dwelling on what prevents you from achieving what you want, you will guarantee yourself a life of personal and professional fulfillment instead of a life of unrealized dreams.

> If you are not achieving the results that you would like, then it's time for you to begin to think differently and put your thoughts into action.

Fall in love with your work. Become organized and competent. Develop a habit of thinking constructively to realize success. You can change your thoughts, your beliefs, and your behavior. When you do, your world will change with you. You have that power. You have that control. What are you going to do? "It" starts with you.

Notes

1. Jack Nicklaus with Ken Bowden, *My Golden Lessons,* (New York: Simon & Schuster, 2002), 51.
2. Denis Waitley, *The Psychology of Winning,* (New York, NY: The Berkley Publishing Group, 1979), 97.
3. Tom Hopkins, *Selling for Dummies* (New York: Hungry Minds, Inc.; 2nd edition, 2001), 38.
4. Maxwell Maltz, M.D., *Psycho-Cybernetics* (Englewood Cliffs, NJ: Prentice Hall, 1960), x.
5. Albert Mehrabian, *Silent Messages: Implicit Communication of Emotions and Attitudes* (Florence, KY: Wadsworth/Cengage, 1980), 77.
6. Richard Bandler, John Grinder, and Virginia Satir, *The Structure of Magic: Volumes 1 and 2,* 1st ed. (Palo Alto, CA: Science and Behavior Books, 1975).
7. Napoleon Hill, *Think and Grow Rich* (New York: Ballantine, 1987), 89.

Resources

The following resources are available at www.BuilderBooks.com:

Gullo, Gina and Angela Rinaldi. *Option Selling for Profit: The Builder's Guide to Generating Design Center Revenue and Profit.* Washington: BuilderBooks.com, 2008.

Nelson, Tara-Nicholle, Esq. *Trillion Dollar Women: Use Your Power to Make Buying & Remodeling Decisions.* Washington: BuilderBooks.com, 2008.

Nowell, William J. *ValueMatch™ Selling for Home Builders: How to Sell What Matters Most.* Washington: BuilderBooks.com, 2008.

Webb, Bill. *Sweet Success in New Home Sales: Selling Strong in Changing Markets.* Washington: BuilderBooks.com, 2006.

Appendix

WORKSHEET 1.1 "It" Factor

1. Write your vision of success on the lines below.

    _____
    _____
    _____
    _____
    _____
    _____
    _____
    _____
    _____
    _____

2. Define your goals and write them down using the prompts below and adding your own:
    a) How much money do you desire?_____
    b) How many sales and closings do you need to have to achieve your financial goal?_____
    c) When do you intend to achieve the goals above?_____
    d) _____
    e) _____

3. Write the details of living out your vision of success. What kind of car do you drive? What clothes do you wear? What awards do you receive? What are your relationships like with other people? See yourself enjoying the success you've attained by reaching the goals above.

4. _____
    _____

5. Write your own daily affirmations using the ones on page XX as a starting point. Read them aloud in the morning and at night before bed.

    _____   _____
    _____   _____
    _____   _____

WORKSHEET 8.1 Features and Benefits

Items	Feature	Bridge	Benefit	Tie-Down
Exterior Front	Our entry doors are all double wide and 8' tall.	This really	makes a grand initial impression.	Don't you agree?
Formal Living Areas	The formal areas include crown molding	which	not only is cosmetically appealing, but it brings attention to the 14' ceilings.	Isn't that appealing?
Family Room	The family room is very convenient to the kitchen.	This will allow you to	be part of the family activities whenever you're in either room.	That's a nice arrangement, don't you think?
Kitchen	The entry from the garage is just steps away from the kitchen.	With this arrangement,	it is really convenient when you come home from shopping.	Wouldn't you agree?
Master Bedroom	Look at the size of this room.	This should	accommodate any furnishings.	Don't you think?

(continued)

WORKSHEET 8.1 Continued

Items	Feature	Bridge	Benefit	Tie-Down
Master Bathroom	This bath is designed in a his-and-hers style.	This allows for	both of you to have your own space, which makes it more comfortable if you are getting ready at the same time.	Wouldn't you agree?
Secondary Bedrooms	Cable, network, and ceiling fan pre-wires are installed in all of the bedrooms.	What this means for you	is that you don't have to hassle with determining which room will be used for what early on in the process.	Isn't that convenient?
Back Yard	The size of this site gives you about 55' from the back of your home to your property line.	So, if you decide	to install a pool now or in the future, you'll have plenty of room.	That resolves your concern, doesn't it?
Garage	The depth of this garage is 25'.	This is important because	regardless of your vehicle choice you will have plenty of room.	Isn't that nice?

WORKSHEET 9.1 Overcoming Resistance

Objection: _____

Anchor that the prospect's concern is
resolved.
- "That resolves that, doesn't it?"
- "This seems to work for you,
  don't you agree?"
- "With this information, you appear
  to be OK with this, isn't that right?"

5 Anchor

Respond to the prospect's issue in a
manner that resolves his concern or
minimizes its importance.

4

Paraphrase your prospect's
concern, acknowledging that you
heard and understand it.

3

Clarify the prospect's real concern.
- "What is it about _____ that
  concerns you?"
- Repeat the concern back to
  the prospect as a question:
  "What do you mean?"

2

Align yourself with the prospect
whenever possible:
- Agree with the truth
      or
- Agree with the odds
      or
- Agree in principle

1

WORKSHEET 12.1 Competition Survey Form

	Obtain Plans	☐
Your Community ————	Obtain List of Home Site Premiums	☐
Competitor	Obtain Neighborhood Layout	☐
Builder ————	Obtain Current Price List	☐
Community ————	Sales Associate Rating (A-C)	☐

Annual Fees:
    Community Development ————
      District if Applicable
    Home Owners' ————
      Association (HOA)

Most Popular Plans
_____
_____

Typical Site Size ————
    Purchaser Incentives _____
    To Be Built _____
    Inventory _____
    Additional Negotiations _____
    _____

Realtor Incentives
    To Be Built _____
    Inventory _____
    Others _____
    _____

Financing Incentives
    Closing Costs Paid _____
    Additional Prepaids Paid _____
    Special Financing Programs _____
    _____

Benefits of the Competitor's Offering over Yours (Include Features and Amenities)
_____
_____
_____
_____

Benefits of Your Offering over Competitor's (Include Features and Amenities)
_____
_____
_____
_____

Index